▼▼▼▼▼▼▼▼▼▼▼▼▼▼▼▼▼▼▼▼▼

THE CAPITAL SINS

The CAPITAL SINS

Seven Obstacles to Life and Love

Gerard P. Weber

ST. ANTHONY MESSENGER PRESS

Cincinnati, Ohio

Nihil Obstat: Rev. Thomas Richstatter, O.F.M., S.T.D.
        Rev. Edward J. Gratsch

Imprimi Potest: The Rev. John Bok, O.F.M., Provincial

Imprimatur: The Most Rev. Carl K. Moeddel, V.G.
        Archdiocese of Cincinnati, March 11, 1997

The *nihil obstat* and *imprimatur* are a declaration that a book is considered to be free from doctrinal or moral error. It is not implied that those who have granted the *nihil obstat* and *imprimatur* agree with the contents, opinions or statements expressed.

Cover and book design by Mary Alfieri
ISBN 0-86716-260-0

Published by St. Anthony Messenger Press
Printed in the U.S.A.

Contents

▼▼▼▼▼▼▼▼▼▼▼▼

Preface

We never know where a leap into the dark will lead us.

In 1987 a group of men came together to talk about what was going on in their lives—work and family, goals and ambitions, death and God, anger and evil. Twice a month a different topic was on the table. One Saturday morning I asked the 30 or so men if they would like to examine the impact of the seven capital sins on their lives. They were intrigued. We used eight short articles from *The Tablet*, a British Catholic weekly, as the basis of our discussions.

The end result of these sessions was not earthshaking, but everyone said they got a lot out of the discussions. They saw more clearly that taken-for-granted behaviors, while not sinful in the usual sense of the word, were detrimental to their efforts to grow in love. After the final session several participants asked to go over the material again in more depth.

I went through this same process with several groups of men and women—with a similar result. This experience suggested that others might also wish to reflect on the "sins" that give birth to other sins and vices. This book is an effort to meet that desire.

I must admit that this interest in the capital sins came as something of a surprise to me. With all the changes of the past decades, I had thought the concept of capital sins had been dismissed as old-fashioned. Sociology and psychology had so many explanations for unloving forms of behavior there seemed little room left for the idea that "out of the heart come evil intentions, murder, adultery, fornication, theft, false witness, slander" (Matthew 15:19).

But I was mistaken. People are seriously struggling with and concerned about the deeper source of the evil inclinations they experience within themselves.

All of a sudden I began noticing references to the "seven deadly sins" popping up in books and articles. Child psychologist Robert Coles wrote in the *New Oxford Review* about his personal experiences with pride, avarice, envy, anger, lust, gluttony and sloth. When *Los Angeles Times* columnist Jack Smith mentioned that "The Seven Deadly Sins" had been played at a music festival in Ojai and that he could not remember a single one of them, readers wrote not only to name the sins but also to lecture him that the idea of sin was not archaic. Not too long after that the movie *SEVEN*, based on the capital sins, was released (November 1995). Interest in these root sins, their meaning and their effects, is still very much alive.

Getting Serious About the Spiritual Life

Reflecting on this material and trying to put it into readable form for a general audience has been the best examination of conscience I have made in years. I have had to look into the nooks and crannies of my life to see where these sins might be hiding. I hope this book will serve a similar function for others.

Deciding what to include and what to leave out has been the hardest part of writing this book. I do not intend an exhaustive or scholarly treatise on the history, nature or origin of the capital sins. Rather, I want to help readers see how the capital sins pop up in everyday life in small as well as in large ways. This book is primarily intended for people who have decided to be more serious about their spiritual lives. Such people have already discarded the obviously harmful ways of thinking and acting. But their housecleaning may not be complete. This book will help readers look at those habits and ways of thinking which, while they may not *seem* to do much harm, indicate that the viruses of the capital sins are still active in some way in their lives.

Looking at the Little Things

This book, then, is an invitation to look not so much at the big things in our lives but at the little ones, the seemingly insignificant habits that keep our love from burning as pure and bright as it might. As you read about and discuss the capital sins and realize how they manifest themselves in so many small ways, you can decide which one or two you need to root out and leave behind as excess baggage on your spiritual journey. Reflection on the capital sins is like watching road signs in order to find the narrow path that leads to life. "Enter through the narrow gate; for the gate is wide and the road is easy that leads to destruction, and there are many who take it. For the gate is narrow and the road is hard that leads to life, and there are few who find it" (Matthew 7:13-14).

Three things help us along this difficult road: The first is *prayer*—especially for enlightenment, wisdom and courage. The second is *knowledge and understanding of ourselves*, of our motives and of our goals in life. The third is *positive action*, doing what we can when we see the capital sins urging us off onto a side road. This book aims to provide that needed knowledge and understanding. The prayer and remedial action are up to the reader.

Using This Book

Reading and reflecting on one chapter at a time is better than reading the book straight through. It would be most helpful to reflect and discuss in a small group of six or eight. A chapter could be read silently by the whole group and then members could share their thoughts. Several reflection starters are offered at the end of each chapter to facilitate this sharing.

The short prayer at the end of each session may be used to close a group session. It can also become a short cry for help whenever we realize that a particular capital sin is infecting our life.

▼▼▼▼▼▼▼▼▼▼▼▼▼▼▼▼▼▼▼▼

CHAPTER ONE

What Are 'Capital Sins'?

▲▲▲▲▲▲▲▲▲▲▲▲▲▲▲▲▲▲▲▲▲▲

My confreres call me a curmudgeon. My good friends say, at times, I am a bit testy. My enemies find me arrogant, argumentative and impossible. I see myself as high-strung and short-fused. For years I confessed the sin of anger while my tongue and pen dripped acid. Then, as I tossed in bed one night after a particularly violent confrontation, a light exploded in my head. "Aha! I see why I got so angry. I felt that the three of them were putting me down and ignoring me!"

Over the next few months I reflected on situations which had occasioned similar outbursts. I came to see that I reacted with anger whenever I felt I was being ignored or put down. This feeling of anger also frequently arose when people did not think the "right" way—*my way*. Taking my cue from Albert Ellis's Rational Emotive Therapy, I began to ask myself his three basic questions: (1) Where is it written in stone that I have to be perfect? (2) Where is it written in stone that everyone has to like me or agree with me? (3) Where is it written in stone that the world has to be fair?

Here are some of the things I began to say to myself with these questions in mind:

- I don't *have* to be perfect. In fact, I *can't* be perfect. I am *not* perfect! Perhaps this is one of the times when I am off base.

- Everyone does not have to like me or agree with me. Maybe this person has good reasons for not liking what I am saying or doing. If the person doesn't have good reasons, the problem is his or hers, not mine.

- The world isn't fair. Even if this situation is unfair, what right have I to think I should fare better than Jesus and all the billions of people who have walked the earth before me and who will trudge along its surface after me?

If I would have reflected on these three questions sooner, I could have responded better when I felt the stirrings of anger. And if I had responded better, my life and the lives around me would have been much less difficult. Over time the obvious answers to these rhetorical questions have become an antacid to calm my agitated response to feelings resulting from my presumption of being put down or ignored.

Now, when I feel the first stirrings of anger at something someone says or does, I try to ask myself, "Is this person really trying to put me down?" If I can see that they are not, my anger ebbs away and I try to respond in a positive way. If I think they are, which rarely happens, I try to think of an appropriate response that lets them know how I feel and that helps me counteract the stirrings of the capital sin of anger.

Name That 'Sin'

Before any of the seven capital sins can be tamed, it must be acknowledged and *named* for what it is. But accurately naming what is going on within us in a given situation is not easy.

We usually can sort out the facts, at least as we see them. We may be able to express the feeling we have. But it is more difficult to see beyond the incident to deeper causes and patterns in our lives and to the source of our sinful actions. Pope Saint Gregory the Great in the sixth century saw the various vices people practice as flowing from seven *heads*—pride, envy, anger, sloth, avarice, gluttony and lust. The Latin word for head or source is *caput*, from which the English word *capital* is derived, hence the seven capital sins. These tendencies are at the head (the source) of all vices and personal sins.

The use of the word *sin* in this context can be very confusing, however. Sin has several different meanings in theological language—and they are more dissimilar than similar. The Hebrew word for sin comes from a word that means "missing the mark." But there are many ways to miss the mark. We can shoot at the wrong target, or completely miss the target at which we aim. We can also hit the target but miss the bull's eye.

But some talk about missing the mark is not about where the arrow lands at all but about the deficit in the bow that causes the arrow to miss the target. Or we can talk about the lack of basic skill in the archer who has a tendency to aim high or pull to the left. In all these cases we are talking about "missing the mark"—but for different reasons.

How does this translate into our traditional vocabulary about sin?

"Mortal sin" is like the arrow that misses the target completely. (It turns one away from God, destroying charity by a serious violation of God's law.) "Venial sin" is like the arrow that hits the target but misses the bull's eye. (It wounds but does not destroy the love of God in one's heart.) Both mortal and venial sins are what we call "personal sins."

When we speak about "original sin" and "capital sins," however, we are speaking about something quite different. Here we are talking about the archer and what motivates the choice of the bow, the arrow and the target.

"Original sin" is something we are born with through no fault of our own. It comes with human nature. Our experience of the evil in people's hearts and lives is proof enough of its lasting effect: Human beings are flawed and have inborn tendencies that are destructive to themselves, to others and to society. Theologians say that the effect of original sin on our lives is that our intellect is darkened and our will is weakened. In other words, we do not always think straight and clearly, nor do we always choose wisely. We can and often do have our facts wrong or incomplete. We can and often do judge impulsively and incorrectly. We can and often do act in destructive ways.

The "capital sins," also called the "deadly sins," are the impulses that cloud our thinking and direct our choices in destructive ways. They are confused, false, inaccurate ways of thinking coupled with a will that is weak when it comes to making hard decisions. This team of impulses destroys the love, the peace and the joy God intended people to have. The capital sins are seven manifestations of original sin at work giving birth to all human vices and all personal sins.

Capital sins can be compared to those genes that carry a propensity for an illness such as cancer or diabetes. The carrier does not automatically have the disease, but an imprint in the cell can allow cancer to develop when the circumstances are right.

Capital sins are also like the dormant viruses we carry. When conditions are right, these seven viruses can cause minor discomfort or explode into serious illness. If we want to control these viruses, it helps to be able to name them accurately. In many cases it will be obvious which one of the seven is at work. In other cases, this is more diffcult. The boundaries between the various capital sins are not clearly defined. More often than not they are like the boundaries between land and water. In some place it is very clear where the land ends and the water begins. In others, as in a marsh or swamp, it is hard to tell what is land and what is water.

When I first had my insight into what was triggering my outbursts, I put the name "anger" on the button that was being pushed and setting me off in a rage. But as I reflected further I became more conscious of how harshly I judged people and of how high my expectations were of them. Gradually it became clear that it was not only anger that punched my button. What was giving *birth* to my outbursts, the *root* cause of my sarcastic remarks, the *fountainhead* of the acid eating my innards was the most deadly of all the capital sins: *pride.*

As I look back now, I can see the value in truly naming

what was eating at me. It has made it easier for me to accept responsibility for my anger when pride stirs it up. I can now see that the source of my uncharitable words and actions was not what other people did but what was happening within me.

Only with this insight have I now begun to think of other less destructive ways to deal with these situations. At times my pen still drips acid and kind words are hard to find. But when I receive the Sacrament of Reconciliation, I now level with my confessor about what is really straining or staining my relationship with God and the People of God.

Claim That Responsibility

My alcoholic friend had just told his counselor and me how much the three-month treatment program had meant to him and how much he had learned about alcoholism. He had apologized to me for all the trouble he had caused, and he told me he was sure he would never take a drink again. I felt relieved and happy.

Then the counselor called me aside. "You know he's lying. He'll be drinking again in three months," the counselor said. He was wrong; it took only two weeks. The counselor knew my friend was still refusing to take responsibility for his drinking. He could name what was causing his life to go on the rocks, but he still put the blame on something outside himself—the stress of his work, a genetic intolerance of alcohol, his drinking companions.

To grow spiritually it is not enough to name the impulses and tendencies that pervert love and prompt us to destructive courses of action. We also need to take ownership of them, to acknowledge that they are our problem and not the problem of someone else. We must *claim* them as ours.

The causes of the capital sins may be and often are beyond our control. They may be the result of psychological problems, of abusive parents, of living in a culture lacking values or steeped in negative ones, even of physical factors such as our genes or a deficiency in certain hormones.

Empirical research into the reasons we think and act as we do makes it clear that we often are not as free as we need to be to combat destructive and addictive habits or ways of thinking. Understanding the impact of psychological problems, abuse in childhood, a bad environment has helped us see that many people who do vicious actions are victims rather than responsible agents. Factors such as these may diminish one's ability to resist the urging of a capital sin, but we still must acknowledge that the destructive tendency is ours and ours alone.

Naming and claiming the disposition to such things as pride, lust or anger is something like admitting that a disease is present in our body. We may not be responsible for the disease being present, but we have to own it as our illness if we want to get well.

The impulses arising from the capital sins can be called *temptations*. We can resist them or succumb to them and, by so doing, develop either good or bad habits, virtues or vices. If we resist the push of the capital sins, we grow in self-control and become more real and more human. If we do not resist and allow the tendency to flower into action, the resulting thoughts, deeds or omissions are sinful to the degree that they are serious and done knowingly and freely. It is not the inclination that is sinful, but what we allow to flow from it.

Tame Those Tendencies

Now and again when I exit from the freeway I see her sitting on the guardrail under the traffic light. Her face is drawn and thin, her dress shabby, her hair gathered with a rubber band at the nape of her neck. She is holding a crude hand-lettered sign of three lines: "Out of work. Two Children. Hungry." Every fifty seconds the light turns from red to green. In that time at least five people waiting for the light to change make decisions about her. Most decide to ignore her. A few hand her a dollar bill. Now and then someone gives her a smile and an encouraging word or makes a disparaging remark. The decisions taken in those few seconds are part of the process of taming or feeding the capital sins in the lives of the people stopped at the light. The incident seems so fleeting, so insignificant that it is hard to relate it to the tug-of-war between the capital sins and the virtues in one's life. Yet it is primarily in these small, daily life encounters that the deadly sins are curbed or fostered.

How might we reflect on the refusal to help a beggar such as the lady sitting at the ramp in order to discover how to curb or tame the power of the capital sins in our life? We could ask what our reaction was and what tendency or inclination was behind that reaction. Was it greed that we did not want to give away money? Was it pride causing us to see the woman as unworthy of attention? Was it sloth that made us indifferent to her plight? Was it anger that she could have allowed herself to get into such a state? If we are serious about enlightening our mind and strengthening our will, we need to name and claim the negative forces in our life and then decide what to do about them.

What we need to do, basically, is to develop the opposite *good* habits: the virtues.

It would be nice if there were seven virtues, each one an antidote to a specific capital sin; but it is not that simple. Theologians do give us a list of seven basic virtues: three theological virtues—faith, hope and charity—by which we direct our actions primarily toward God, and the four cardinal virtues—justice, fortitude (courage) temperance and prudence from which flow a multitude of other virtues such as chastity, modesty, generosity, truthfulness, meekness, magnanimity, sincerity and so on. But it is easy to see that in dealing with the stirrings of a capital sin, one may need to develop several of these virtues.

A driver in a car at the stoplight at the top of the ramp may need faith and love to see the woman sitting there as a child of God as well as a spirit of generosity to offer her help. Merely saying, "I'll not pass her by again," usually does not work because it is too easy to forget our resolve or to think of a good reason not to keep it when we drive up that ramp some weeks later.

Taming a capital sin is achieved best by practicing a contrary virtue at the time. In this case it might be the virtue of generosity. However, if we pass her by but reflect on the incident later, we can decide what we will do the next time we see her or someone in her position. We can form a picture in our mind imagining ourself opening the window and giving her a dollar. Later when we come upon a similar situation, this positive image may counteract the impulse to ignore the person.

If a fleeting incident such as this causes us to reflect on our motives and inclinations, it is also helpful to talk it over with a trusted friend or with a wise spiritual companion to see how it might be affecting our life in other situations. Often such a person can help us change our way of thinking and act in a more positive way. Finally, as with all situations in life, laying what we discover at the feet of God and asking for divine enlightenment and strength is helpful in overcoming the infection caused by any of the capital sins.

The struggle with the seven deadly sins begins when we are born and will end only when we die. They attack with more or less frequency and with more or less virulency many times during the day. Reflection on these attacks should prompt us frequently to cry out with Paul, "For I do not do the good I want, but I do the evil I do not want" (Romans 7:19). The realization that we are not perfect, that we do sin and that often we seem to be overwhelmed by these vicious inclinations is the basis of humility and of our total dependence on God. The effort we make to deal with and control these tendencies forges our character.

If we constantly give into them, our hearts grow cold, our vision of the good and beautiful grows dim, our search for God grows listless. If, on the other hand, we courageously battle them, we may fail at times, but because we are trying our hearts will gradually glow with more love. The true and the beautiful will be seen from a new perspective, and God will be found not at the end of a long search but walking beside us all along.

For Reflection

1. Complete the following sentence with your own metaphor or comparison: Capital sins are like...

2. In what way do you see the capital sins as different from original sin and from personal sin?

3. Recall and share a time in your life when you felt that something was not going right, and you were able to put your finger on it and name it. But were you able to claim it, to acknowledge that it was your responsibility and no one else's? And what did you do to tame it?

Prayer

FATHER OF LOVE AND MERCY, we are weak and prone to sin. Cleanse our desires, enlighten our minds and strengthen our wills that we may grow in virtue. We ask this through Christ our Lord.

CHAPTER TWO

▼▼▼▼▼▼▼▼
Pride
▲▲▲▲▲▲▲▲

A sculptor invited a neighbor in to see his small clay model for a bronze statue of a young woman. Her head was held high, her back straight. Her outstretched arms held an infant for all to see. The sculptor asked the neighbor's opinion. He walked around it two or three times, squinted at it from below and above. Finally he said, "That's a mighty proud young woman."

The sculptor was delighted. "That's what I wanted," he exclaimed, "a really proud Madonna."

The sculptor had a right to be proud, too. He did not see his statue as competing with Michelangelo's *Pieta*, but he had given form to an exalted ideal and others were able to recognize it. (The bronze cast of that statue now stands on the front lawn of a Catholic high school for girls.)

Mary, the sculptor's inspiration, certainly had a right to be proud. She realized that, by giving birth to the son of the Most High, she played a pivotal role in a great historical moment. "Surely, from now on will all generations call me blessed" (Luke 1:48b).

But this proud Mary was also humble in the most perfect sense of the word. She did not take the credit: "My soul magnifies the Lord,...for he has looked with favor on the lowliness of his servant" (1:46-48a). Without shrinking from acknowledging the blessings that were hers, she attributed them to God, not to her own human efforts.

Humility and pride go hand in hand. We cannot understand the one without understanding the other. True humility is based on a realistic self-esteem and self-knowledge. A humble person sees herself as a creature of the

Almighty—loved, talented but imperfect. A humble person recognizes and acknowledges not only his limitations, but also his talents and achievements. True humility is the acknowledgment that all we have and all we have achieved are unmerited gifts from God.

Mighty Proud and Pretty Humble

In the popular mind humility is often associated with a hangdog look, with an "aw shucks, it ain't much" attitude, with a downplaying of one's real talents and abilities, with always deferring to the wishes of another. But such attitudes are actually a *false* humility, a refusal to see what is good in ourselves and to acknowledge it as a gift from God.

It may sound corny when a ballplayer or boxer attributes his success to God, as did Reggie White on international television right after his team, the Green Bay Packers, won the 1997 Super Bowl. But if the person is sincere, this is an expression of true humility.

False humility is refusing to acknowledge the dignity and gifts God has given us. It often manifests itself in a feeling of uneasiness at being complimented or in the inability to accept a deserved accolade. This false humility can be an expression of a poor self-image or a lack of self-esteem. But it can just as easily be a cover-up for the capital sin of pride: One can be proud of one's humility!

Just as there is a true humility, there is also a true and legitimate pride. True pride acknowledges our abilities and successes and lets us see ourselves for what we are—beings created by a good and loving God.

Our culture pushes many different types of programs to improve self-image, assertiveness or self-esteem. Such programs encourage pride in self and believing one can accomplish the impossible dream.

It is true that every single person has talents and abilities, that every single life is of inestimable value. But attributing our abilities and value to our own efforts without acknowledging that, ultimately, they are due to the goodness of God is a form of lying to ourselves.

This lie gives rise to *false* pride. The ancients called it vainglory—an exaggerated estimate of one's abilities. In talking about pride it is always necessary to distinguish between rightful self-esteem (true pride) and vainglory (false pride). When speaking of the capital sins, pride refers to that refusal to admit and to be satisfied with one's limitations. It is legitimate self-love gone awry.

It is not too difficult to detect this false pride in the woman who dismisses anyone who disagrees with her as "stupid." Or in the well-appointed business executive who looks down at those in less fashionable suits or cars.

But pride shows itself in more subtle ways as well: not listening to what other people are saying because we are so eager to express our own ideas; fishing for compliments about how one is dressed or how youthful one looks; doing *The New York Times* crossword puzzle *in ink*.

Humility, on the one hand, is the honest acceptance of the human condition. It recognizes limitations. It keeps aspirations and dreams reasonable, within the bounds of our abilities.

Pride, on the other hand, is a lie. It causes us to overestimate our abilities, to exaggerate our achievements, to inflate our importance. Like a magician, it makes one see what is not really there at all—or to see what is there in a way that is distorted.

It is a lie, for example, that anyone with hard work, the proper education and some breaks can achieve whatever he or she sets out to do. The truth is that a person may not have the necessary intelligence or aptitude to realize a particular dream. Most young people who dream of becoming professional athletes never make it because their hopes and dreams are not based on the requisite physical and mental abilities. They have not made a truthful, a humble, assessment of themselves.

Humility does not suggest that we not try to reach for the stars and do better than we think we can. It does keep us, however, from lying to ourselves about what we actually are

13

capable of doing. It does keep us from attempting the impossible just because a project seems so good or the rewards so great.

Pride seduces us to live in a world of fantasy. It causes blind spots in our view of reality. It overlooks, avoids, forgets and rationalizes the real obstacles and barriers that we face. It causes us to ignore the obvious and to select and focus only on the things we want to see or believe.

Pride is insidious. It can even camouflage as humility. True humility admits that we are not perfect, that we fail and sin many times a day. But pride may well be doing its deceptive work in the scrupulous person who goes over the same material time and time again trying to find the slightest trace of sin in his or her actions or thoughts.

False pride is the basis of the individualism that does "my own thing" without regard for the responsibility one has to others, to their feelings, to their rights. It causes one to reject authority if that authority does not agree with one's ideas of what is right, correct or necessary for community life. The motto of the sixties—"Never trust anyone over thirty"—is an example of the type of pride that sees its own ideas and experience as the norm for reality and action.

Humility is willing to take a backseat, to allow another to shine. Pride, on the other hand, cannot bear to see another in first place. It distorts the healthy sense of competition that seeks to find better ways by which politics, technology or business can work for the benefit of all. Pride leads to dirty tricks and unethical tactics in the halls of government and in the marketplace.

In sports, pride justifies doing anything to win, whether it's taking steroids or physically attacking a competitor. Its motto: "If winning isn't the purpose of the game, what is?"

Proud people think they are—or at least could be—outstanding in all tasks undertaken. They look down upon, perhaps despise, others engaged in similar efforts. They see others' accomplishments as petty in comparison to their own—or at least in comparison to what they think they would do if in the same situation.

Here are some other examples to help name the ways the capital sin of pride manifests itself in human life:

The humble person acknowledges talents, successes and failures, neither seeking nor placing high value on praise from others. The proud person seeks praise and first place and is miserable when denied it.

The humble person attributes achievements and virtues to God and accepts personal responsibility for moral lapses. The proud person attributes achievements and virtues to personal powers and blames moral lapses on someone or something beyond one's control.

The humble person is never ashamed of his or her family or community. The proud person often seeks to hide, ignore or embellish a humble background in order to seem better than he or she is.

A humble person has solid self-esteem that holds up well in adversity. A proud person is always seeking to bolster self-image by taking credit for more than is fair.

Humility is the basis for the self-love and self-respect we need in order to be able to love others and God. Pride sneaks in when that self-esteem is not based on reality, when it takes credit for qualities it does not possess or for superficial or unimportant honors or possessions.

We pay a high price for allowing pride to color, direct and motivate our thoughts, feelings and actions. While humility leads to greatness of soul, pride leads to the shriveling up of the soul. This shriveling comes from defensively circling the wagons to protect the inflated self and keep others out. As time goes on, that circle gets more and more difficult to penetrate.

The ultimate price of pride is *alienation*. It cuts us off from our true self, from others and from God.

The people who gathered to build the tower at Babel in order to make a proud name for themselves ended up not even being able to speak to one another. In addition to a tower, their pride built walls of separation between peoples of different tribes. Those same kind of walls rise brick by brick whenever we give in to a prideful impulse. To see how actions dictated by pride cut a person off from other people, recall how you've felt and reacted to a person who acts in an arrogant, insolent, egotistical, haughty or condescending manner. You probably avoided the "know it all" at all costs.

Think of the hurts and divisions in families caused by members who think only of themselves, of their feelings, of their desires. Sisters do not talk with one another because one said something that hurt the other's feelings. A father will not allow a son or daughter into the house until the child apologizes for some action.

Blocking out, walling off another person is always a sign of pride. The father of the Prodigal Son was a humble man. He went out to meet the returning profligate and embraced him. When the father heard that the older son was miffed, he also went out to him to make peace. Pride would have prompted the father in both cases to stand on his dignity and rights as the head of the family and insist the young men come to him. But he humbly allowed no walls to stand between him and his sons.

The behaviors that arise from pride distance us from God. Adam and Eve did not do anything that seemed earthshaking to them. They merely ate a piece of fruit. But by taking just one bite, they were refusing to acknowledge their limitations and the supremacy of God.

The Bible says that God placed an angel with a revolving fiery sword to guard the way to the tree of life. This is a most powerful image of the alienating effect of pride on our relationship to God. The sword of that angel flashes and whirls each time we give into a prideful impulse.

The definition of serious sin is this: a break in our loving, obedient relationship to God. Because so much emphasis has been placed on actions that break the commandments, people tend not to appreciate how attitudes spawned by pride cause them to hold up a hand and tell God not to come any closer or to leave their lives.

This attitude of independence gets expressed in slogans such as, "I'll do it my way"; "No one has the right to tell me what is right or wrong"; "I and I alone have to plan for and

16

provide for my future." These slogans can be a healthy expression of personal responsibility. But if carried to their ultimate conclusion of denying dependence on God, they are an expression of false pride.

Besides alienating us from others and from God, pride alienates us from our real self. It clouds our mind and judgment with illusions and misapprehensions so that we become less capable of dealing with life and making wise decisions. Pride takes a great deal of the joy out of the here and now. Instead of recognizing and enjoying the gifts and achievements we have, the proud person is always looking for something more—more recognition, a better position, more power.

Humility brings contentment with our gifts and achievements. It helps us see ourselves more clearly and more realistically and, therefore, we become more capable of making sound decisions. Because humble people realize their utter dependence on God and their interdependence with the entire human race, they are not so likely to be seduced by the prospect of honor, position and power at the expense of their relationship to God and their ultimate destiny.

'I Am Proud!'

Once we have named the virus of pride, it is important to acknowledge its presence in our lives. The first step that people in Alcoholics Anonymous must take is to admit that they are alcoholics. The first step in confronting the obstacle of pride is to say, "I am a proud person."

It is relatively easy to spot instances of pride in other people's actions, words and attitudes. Yet pride is constantly nudging us to put too great a value on our own dignity, abilities or position. We have the ability to camouflage our attitudes and justify our actions by using words that sound noble, good and honorable. We often fail to see the pride behind our angry word, offensive remark, or disparaging comment. We focus on the failure of the other person and refuse to acknowledge our own contribution to an

17

interpersonal problem.

We all prefer not to look into our own hearts to see whether it is our inflated ego that is causing us to strike out at another, to contradict others especially in inconsequential things, to put others down, to twist every conversation around to our interests, to find fault with whatever another might do. The virus of pride is at work in all these ways we deal with others. We do not realize that these habits reflect the need always to be right, to be the best, to know things better than others, to be in charge.

With pride as with all the capital sins, we tend to think of their obvious and obnoxious manifestations and say, "Well, I don't act *that* way." But little habits may be an indication that pride is present. It is right and proper, for example, to dress decently for an occasion, but dressing in order to be the center of attention at a party at least suggests that the virus of pride is stirring. The same is true of deliberately arriving late for a party, meeting or a class so that our entrance will be noticed. Chattering constantly and interrupting others may be just a nervous habit manifesting our insecurity, but it can also be an indication that we think that no one else has anything worthwhile to say.

Neglecting to say thank you for gifts we receive or for an everyday kindness may be caused by any number of things, but it can also be a sign of pride. Are we are so self-centered that we take these things for granted and do not acknowledge the kindness and love behind them?

How can we become more sensitive to the ways the virus of pride infects us? We need to reflect on how we relate to other people and on what this reveals about our opinion of ourselves.

One spur to such reflection is to tally daily the number of times we uses the words *I*, *me*, *my* and *mine* in conversation. Then we need to ask *why*. There may be many reasons why we keep ourselves up front in conversation. Maybe we feel insecure or unappreciated and are unconsciously putting ourselves center stage. The important question here is whether such attempts to make "me" and "mine" the center of the conversational world is an indication that pride is at work in us.

Another reflection technique is to recall whether and how often friends use adjectives denoting pride when speaking of us. J.I. Rodale's book *The Synonym Finder* has seventy-six variations on pride, sixteen of which begin with *self*: self-satisfied, self-important, self-contented, etc. These and other adjectives—such as conceited, proud, arrogant, imperious, cocky, ostentatious, boastful—can give a clue to what others may be reading in our character.

A third way to detect the virus of pride is to ask another person for assistance. Someone with whom we can talk openly and honestly can help us name any uneasiness we feel in the way we think and act and, if appropriate, claim it as pride.

Finally, of course, we can ask God's help. We can pray for enlightenment about the underlying tendencies that keep us from being the person we want to be.

Practicing Humility

Having named and claimed pride, the next question is what to do about it. One thing that does not work is simply to say, "I'll never do that again!" This resolution might last through one or two situations, but then we do it again. If pride is a habit that pops up with some regularity, the most effective thing to do is to practice the opposite virtue of humility.

This does not mean going around saying, "I am no good. I am a failure. I am nothing." It means accepting ourselves for our strengths *and* weaknesses. Humility values the talents we actually have but does not try to appropriate those we do not have or have only in a flawed form. A realistic and honest love of self realizes that we are loved by God who sees good in us. We accept that love even though we recognize that we are not perfect and must continually try to do better. Trappist Vincent Dwyer says that on Judgment Day God will not ask whether we *succeeded* but whether we *tried*.

A realistic appraisal of our own talents and flaws also

helps us accept and value the talents and accomplishments of others. When pride prompts us to criticize another, to push ourselves forward, it is helpful to look for and acknowledge the other's *good* qualities. Honest self-love is based on humility and on respect for ourselves; but it also leads to respect for others.

Simple actions can help us tame our pride and cultivate a humble spirit: taking a back seat in a situation, allowing others to lead, listening to and respecting what others are saying, asking advice from those who may be better informed, doing the jobs that others do not want, serving instead of being served.

And, finally, we can read the Gospels. Meditating on how Jesus regarded others (who obviously were not as perfect as he was) and noticing how he treated them can be a powerful incentive to practice humility and overcome pride.

For Reflection

1. What differences do you see between a healthy self-esteem and vainglory?

2. What are some of the little ways you see false pride in the words, actions or attitudes of people? In what ways do even these small manifestations build walls between people?

3. Recall a person whom you see as truly humble. List the characteristics of that person that indicate humility to you.

Prayer

LORD, you resist the proud. Help me know what I am truly capable of doing and of not doing. Give me the wisdom to accept my limitations as well as to acknowledge the gifts you have given me. This I ask in the name of Jesus.

CHAPTER THREE

Envy

When I was a young boy we played a game called king of the hill. The hill was a pile of dirt dumped into a vacant lot near our house. The king was the boy who managed to make it to the top and fend off the rest of us who were trying to take his place. When the game was over we were usually laughing because we had such a good time.

Once in a while, however, one of the fellows would get angry and sulk because he had been unable to dethrone the reigning king. He experienced a sense of inferiority, of failure. Perhaps he even felt a twinge of animosity toward the one who *was* king of the hill that day. He was envious of that stronger boy who had managed to get to the top and stay there.

Envy is the pain that comes from perceiving another as possessing an object, a quality or a status that we don't possess but would like to. Like the other capital sins, it isn't easy to identify. In that vacant lot of my childhood, it was camouflaged as the desire to win the game, to be champ.

Feeling 'Less' Because Another Has 'More'

Part of the difficulty in identifying envy stems from the fact that it is a perversion of a perfectly good and noble aspect of self-love: the desire to be the best person we can be. True self-love is based on an accurate assessment of who we are and what we can and cannot do. It accepts the fact that we are not gods and that the talents we do have are individual and limited. Trial and error help us discover things we can do well, things we can do only moderately well and things we

21

can't do at all.

Desiring and striving to emulate the qualities of another can be a good and healthy spur to our own growth. The energy behind words like *want, desire, long for, wish for, fancy* or *crave* can motivate us to throw ourselves wholeheartedly into the effort to develop our talents to the fullest. In the writings of the saints we frequently find such words used to express their ardent desire to love God and their neighbor with their whole heart and soul.

Take the story of the young woman who wanted to be a TV news producer. She knew that at all the stations in her city the news was written and produced by men. She nevertheless applied at a station where not even one woman worked in the newsroom in any capacity at all. She was offered—and took— a job as a typist. But in a short time she managed to show that she could write well. She became the first woman newswriter at the station and then moved on to a larger station where she became the first woman news producer. She was motivated by a healthy appreciation of her own talents and ambition, not by envy of the men who held these jobs.

Envy is different from not being satisfied with who and what we are. Dissatisfaction with ourselves can cause us to strive to develop the talents we do have or to come to a more realistic appraisal of our own unique gifts. Envy is the pain we feel as we look at another's talents, possessions, honors or position and conclude that we are somehow *less* because the other person has something we lack. Our self-esteem suffers; we feel dejected and resentful of the other's good fortune.

The seeds of envy are planted early in life. Somehow we get the message that we are not quite good enough, that there is something wrong with us because we are not like all the others. Friends and even parents compare us with other babies and siblings. School compares our achievements to norms and to those of other students. As adults our ability, our work, our position is constantly compared not only with others but with the bottom line. These comparisons—when detrimental—can cause us to think less of ourselves and to be envious of others.

Our self-esteem is attacked when we are passed up for a promotion or someone else gets the job for which we applied. We feel a jab at our ego when our dress or suit is not as fashionable as those worn by others at an event. Envy is a sneaky virus ready to infect practically any contact we have with others.

Comparing ourselves to others is good when it stimulates us to try harder, to do better, to reach a goal. Comparisons can, in fact, be a blessing if they motivate us to take stock of how well we are developing the gifts we do have.

For many years I coauthored books with another priest who had a clear and concise writing style. My sentences, in contrast, took up half a page and broke all the rules for clear writing. Over the years I have tried to improve by using his writing as a model. I constantly ask myself, "Am I saying this as clearly as Jake would?" Comparing my style with his has been an inspiration for me to do better.

Comparing ourselves to others can, however, lead to envy and unethical behavior. The first sin described in Scripture had its roots in the pride of Adam and Eve; but the second sin was born of envy.

Cain was envious because God accepted his brother Abel's offering and refused his own. "So Cain was very angry, and his countenance fell" (Genesis 4:5). In other words, Cain's opinion of himself fell. He was dejected and angry. Instead of looking into himself to see how he might improve his offering and make it acceptable to God, he killed his brother.

Discovering that we fail to compare favorably with another can cause us, like Cain, to feel bitter, angry, resentful, critical. It can lead us to vicious and cruel actions.

A scientist engaged in some esoteric research discovered that the refrigerators in which he kept his cultures were being turned off. Once or twice could have been the result of a mistake, but after the third incident he realized that someone was trying to sabotage his project. Envy was at work.

Envy can also be expressed in little ways: being cross or irritable with the person we envy; focusing on the other's faults and trying to bring him or her down to our level;

clamming up in our rival's presence. Or we may cry. That is what one very intelligent and competitive young woman did whenever grades were posted and she was not first or second in her class.

Envy locks us into a false notion of ourselves. It hardens our heart and blocks our mind from accepting who and what we truly are. Envy prods us to locate our value *in what other people are* instead of *in what we are*. It nourishes a continual regret for what we want but cannot have. It fosters meanness and pettiness—even encouraging us to spread untruths about others. Envy is depressed at another's good fortune and rejoices at misfortune.

Envy builds walls between us and those we envy. It leads us to become critical of them and makes it difficult, if not impossible, for us to recognize and acknowledge their achievements. It keeps us from affirming the goodness in the other. Thus Dante's *Divine Comedy* pictures the envious man sitting with sealed eyes unable to see anything.

Envy also walls us off from God. It makes us feel that life—God—has cheated us and so we are not thankful for what we have been given. It robs us of our ability to rejoice in God's goodness and generosity to others and to ourselves.

Sometimes the pain caused by envy arises from a longing for the abilities and successes of another. When we realize that we are not and cannot be as charming, as good looking, as popular, as smart, as successful as someone else, our sense of self is threatened or even diminished. And the sneaky hand of false pride is often at work behind the scenes preventing us from acknowledging that pain for what it is, attributing it instead to another cause such as injustice, lack of opportunity or just plain bad luck.

But the pain of envy can also arise from greedily longing for others' possessions. A concert violinist may desire a rare Stradivarius just like the one owned by a guest soloist. When a feeling of sadness overcomes him whenever he hears the guest playing, envy is at work. When, roiled up inside at the sight of the other opening her violin case, he makes

24

disparaging remarks about her ability, the virus of envy is creating a full-blown infection in his soul.

'I Want the Violin!'

Each of us at times will have a craving for someone else's Stradivarius. We may desire clothes, a sports car, a larger house, new furniture or any of the thousands of things or experiences that make up modern life. We worry that we cannot take the kind of vacations our neighbors take. We are envious of the person in the office who has an "in" with the boss.

It is often difficult to identify these thoughts and feelings as envy, however, because they are cloaked in what seem to be legitimate desires for the improvement of our life.

But when the desire to have what another has gives rise to discord, friction, resentment, even a feeling of sadness or of being inadequate, a perverted form of self-love is at work. This kind of desire often leads to lying, backbiting and even underhanded efforts to acquire whatever is desired.

When a person wants what another has and tries to take it away, not only is the infection of envy full-blown, but the virus of greed has been activated as well. Solomon faced this combination of envy and greed when two women came to him each claiming a newborn baby as her own.

Solomon, realizing that the real mother would give up her claim so that the child might live, ordered the baby to be cut in two and a half given to each woman. When the real mother immediately ceded her claim to prevent the slaughter, Solomon gave the baby to her.

The Bible does not tell us what happened to the other woman who was motivated by the most deadly form of envy. She wanted to take something away from another not just because she wanted it, but because she did not want the other to have it at all. She was willing to destroy the child in this envious spirit: "If I cannot have it neither will you!"

Envy fools us into believing that if the other person no longer has what we desire, then we will feel better about ourselves. Envy says that our worth increases when another has less.

Envy affects social groups, institutions and cultures as well as individuals. It feeds on the inequality of wealth in our society that produces the "haves" and the "have nots." This envy is easily named when a ghetto mob burns the store of a recent immigrant who has managed to put together a few dollars and go into business. It may be more difficult to identify when a riot, such as the one in Los Angeles triggered by perceptions of police brutality, rips through a city destroying the very neighborhoods where rioters live. The surface cause may be a perceived injustice, but also active in the mass psyche is an envy on the part of those passed over by the American dream.

Envy accompanied by greed is also the cause of much international and civil strife. One country or one group wants the resources, the power, the wealth of another. The effort to take these by force is seldom identified as an exercise in envy and greed. It is usually cloaked in the noble sentiments of protecting one's national interests or preserving one's ethnic identity.

Envy surfaces in so many ways that not one but *two* commandments forbid it. "Neither shall you covet your neighbor's wife. Neither shall you desire your neighbor's house, or field, or male or female slave, or ox, or donkey, or anything that belongs to your neighbor" (Deuteronomy 5:21).

Scripture tells several classic stories of envy. David and Bathsheba and Ahab and Naboth are but two.

Uriah had a beautiful wife whom David coveted. We usually think of lust as what motivated David to take Bathsheba and murder Uriah, but envy was also present. Uriah had something David did not have and wanted. It was envy that led David to have a good soldier killed (2 Samuel 11:1-26).

Ahab, king of Samaria, fell into a deep depression when Naboth would not sell him the vineyard he wanted. The king, envious of that plot of land, would not eat or drink until he could have it. Ahab's wife, Jezebel, had poor Naboth

26

murdered so the king could get the land (2 Kings 21:1-16).

Neither David nor Ahab took ownership of the envy they felt until a prophet confronted them and pronounced God's punishment. Only then did they acknowledge the motive for their sins.

To keep envy from leading us to do serious harm to others and to ourselves, we need to identify correctly our impulses to begrudge others their talents or possessions; we need to honestly acknowledge that we feel envious. Only then can we tame the demon of envy lurking in the closet of our soul.

Being Satisfied With 'Enough'

While I was preparing an article on envy for a series in *St. Anthony Messenger*, I read a previous article on pride written some months before. I was struck by two or three neat wordplays and the clever way it ended. I was thinking, "That's not bad."

But when I looked at the manuscript I had sent to the editor, I did not find those wordplays or the clever ending. My immediate reaction: "My work is not good enough. She had to change it. Why can't I turn a phrase like that?"

Feeling inadequate is often a good first indication that envy is at work pinching our heart. I might have easily responded by getting down on myself as an inadequate writer. But I decided to take a cue from Solomon Schimmel's book, *The Seven Deadly Sins*. I looked at the positive side. Over 900 of those 1,000 words were mine. "Not bad," I thought. Then I reread the article and appreciated the editor's contributions. I said to myself, "I'm lucky to have an editor who is so good and who puts time and effort into polishing my writing. Some editors merely change commas and tenses. This editor cares!" Envy slunk back into its dank and foul den—at least for the time being.

Humility—accepting ourselves for what we are—is a powerful protection against envy. It helps us accept the fact that we are not perfect (but who is?), that we do not have all the things we want (but who does?). Humility also helps us stay focused on the important truth: that each of us is individually loved by God who is calling us to be the best we can be.

God calls us to be *the best that we can be*—not to be somebody else's best. Realizing this can help us tame envy.

God created us all equal in some sense, but we cannot all do and achieve the same things. We must rejoice in our diversity instead of being envious of those who have talents other than our own. To do this we must begin by becoming conscious of our own talents, limited as they may be. God wants all of us to have the things necessary for a secure and human life, but that does not mean that everyone should have *all* that everyone else has. Being satisfied with "enough" and not desiring "more" is the road to taming envy.

When the virus of envy invades the heart, it becomes a habit that can affect one relationship or several. As with any other infection, the sooner one spots the symptoms and begins to use the appropriate antidotes, the easier it will be to cure or at least control.

Envy can be tamed by honest reflection, self-knowledge, self-acceptance and charity. Unfortunately, many people in our busy world today do not seem to have time to reflect and ask themselves the crucial questions about what is going on in their lives. In the groups I have worked with, I have found that folks are good at discerning the *facts* of a situation but have difficulty seeing the connections between events and the *motives* behind them. Therefore they have difficulty naming and claiming capital sins such as envy.

So if you detect any of the symptoms of envy listed previously, it would be healthy to find a quiet spot and take some time to (1) name what is going on inside, (2) take a reading of self-worth and self-acceptance and (3) determine in what ways envy is manifesting itself. The following questions are grouped to help with each task.

First, try to name what is going on inside:

- Does recognizing that another person has abilities or possessions you do not have and would like to have disturb your peace of mind and make you feel sad or dejected?

- Why is it important to you to be like that other person or to have what that person has?

- How do you feel about and speak about that person?

- How important is it in the light of eternity to be like that person or to have what that person has?

Second, take a reading on self-worth and self-acceptance:

- What makes you worthwhile?

- What good qualities, talents or achievements do you have that the other person may not have?

- How well do you accept your limitations and weaknesses?

Third, determine in what ways envy is manifesting itself:

- What mean things is envy causing you to say or do?

- What kind of person are you becoming because of this envy?

- In what way is envy coloring your view of yourself, of the other person and of life?

Finally, develop a positive outlook and strategy:

- What are the benefits you have enjoyed because you do not have the same talents or possessions the other has?

- What does the fact that you are envious tell you about yourself?

- In what way can you turn this desire to be like another into an asset in your life?

- How often do you thank God for these benefits and for the fact that you are unique and not like the other?

Such reflection, while helpful, will not in itself kill the virus of envy. The ultimate antidote lies in realizing that we are good, worthwhile and lovable and in accepting and liking ourselves for what we are. Related to this is the effort to do the little things that develop envy's opposite virtue, charity: speaking well of the other, rejoicing in the other's success, sincerely complimenting the other.

Charity surrounds and stifles envy because it sees the successes, the happiness, the security of the other as being as important, if not more important, than my own. How can we truly say that we love another if, in our hearts, we are saying that the person's gifts, successes, position, even the good that person does should be ours?

Saint Paul gave the cure for envy in his advice to the Romans: "Rejoice with those who rejoice, weep with those who weep. Live in harmony with one another; do not be haughty, but associate with the lowly; do not claim to be wiser than you are" (Romans 12:15-16).

For Reflection

1. *Sometimes it helps to understand a capital sin such as envy by looking at it from a totally different, even whimsical, viewpoint. For example, to what animal, bird, fish or reptile would you liken envy? Why?*

2. *How would you describe envy in your own words?*

3. *Why do you think envy robs one of peace of mind, joy and tranquility?*

4. *What simple, practical things can you suggest to help a person name, claim and tame envy?*

Prayer

LORD, you rejoice in the talents and achievements of even the least gifted of your children. You put no value on the gold and silver some people pile up. Please touch our hearts to rejoice in the talents of others. Help us realize that our true value lies not in what we accomplish or have but in being loved by you and sharing that love with others.

▼▼▼▼▼▼▼
Anger
▲▲▲▲▲▲▲

During the Cold War, the United States Air Force monitored information from as far away as Turkey, always alert for signs that missiles or bombers were on their way from Russia to the United States. When a suspicious blip appeared on a screen, it was immediately evaluated and a decision made whether to ignore it, alert a fighter plane or send a squadron of B-52s.

Deep inside each of us is a similar command center on 24-hour alert for threats to our well-being. The feeling on guard duty is anger. When danger—physical or emotional, real or imagined—threatens, this inner watchdog sounds an alarm and we immediately prepare to fight or to flee.

So far so good. That's the way we are made and the way the emotion of anger is supposed to serve us. How does the normal emotion of anger become the deadly sin of anger? It's all in how we react once the alarm is sounded.

Sentry of the Self

The inner watchdog of anger, the sentry of the self, reacts differently in each person depending on individual temperament. In some folks it is easygoing, seldom seeing anything as a real threat. In others it is ready to sound the alarm at the slightest provocation.

One day a Chinese priest I lived with was trying to jump-start his car and did something wrong. The battery blew up. All he said was, "Well, look at that!" Another time the gas tank fell off the car as he was driving. He calmly called the rectory and asked us what to do.

His inner watchdog did not go on alert for little things. People like this usually have a positive, upbeat view of people and life. But the same set of experiences for another person could have tripped the alarm bell of anger immediately.

Besides determining how slowly or quickly the inner watchdog sounds the alarm, our basic temperament also determines the style in which we react once the bell starts ringing. Some people immediately run for the bomb shelter. Their first reaction to threat is to flee, physically or emotionally. The "doormat wife" who never disagrees with her husband, the taciturn husband who will never discuss family problems because it usually leads to an argument—their instinct is to avoid life's unpleasantness.

Other folks go on full alert. They are ready to strike physically, confront verbally, slam doors, break things—even wash windows or clean the house to vent their anger.

Why some temperaments are more phlegmatic and others extremely excitable is the focus of ongoing research. But the fact that environmental and physical factors shape our temperament and therefore our response to threat does not mean we cannot control anger or its unsavory children: vengeance, hate, rage, resentments, insults, rancor, quarrels. It does mean, however, that some of us find it a greater challenge than others.

The important point is this: No matter what our temperament, no matter how quickly or slowly our inner sentry sounds the alarm, and no matter whether we are predisposed to fight or to flight, we can decide how we are going to respond to the emotional juices once they start to flow.

Anger is an emotion, a feeling, and as such is neither good nor bad. It's the way it influences a person's thinking or behaving that is good or bad. And it can have a deadly effect. That's why wise men over the centuries have listed anger as one of the capital sins, a fountainhead spewing forth all sorts of harm to the individual, to others and to society.

Some writers in the past have maintained that anger can

never be justified even in a just cause. I suspect they would like to rewrite Scripture so that Jesus sits down calmly with the merchants in the Temple and quietly convinces them to take their money tables and animals out of the holy place. Most authors, however, speak of a "just anger" that can be a source of good when it impels us to defend a person who is being attacked or when it motivates us to crusade against injustice. Anger at injustice can lead us to take positive steps to right existing wrongs.

A woman volunteering in a retirement center saw the way the elederly were being taken advantage of because they did not know the law or because they had no one to help them with all the red tape. This angered her. Even though she was sixty herself, she went to law school, passed the bar and devoted her efforts to help the elderly get their due.

Yet even a "just anger" must always be tempered by mercy, compassion and nonviolence. Since anger often blinds people to their own lack of charity and justice, it can be dangerous to seek justice through violent means.

In the vast majority of cases anger inspires cutting words, frozen silence, hatred, physical or psychological violence—all of which are bad. Anger's harm is usually easy to spot when physical violence occurs. The psychological harm it does to others is not always easy to see.

Being the frequent object of a parent's or teacher's angry outbursts can contribute to a child's poor self-esteem and sense of worthlessness. Adult targets of anger can, at the very least, experience upset, hurt or even become angry themselves.

No matter how justified we feel in our anger, unless it is controlled and tempered, it will surely harm *us*. Loss of sleep, headaches, stomach upsets, ulcers or diabetic flare-ups—all can be the result of the inner turmoil anger produces.

But anger also harms us by distorting our perception of reality. Anger acts like the blinders on a horse. An angry person cannot see anything but the cause of the hurt. How many people have left the Church, given up the practice of their faith because they were angry with what a priest said or did? They cannot see past the person to the message and presence of Christ.

Anger makes it difficult to see what is good in a situation. It can cause us to ignore the progress a child or a spouse is making in changing behavior. It blinds us to comprehending the reasons behind what another said or did. In other words, anger usually makes the one who is angry more miserable than the one at whom the anger is directed.

Beside harming the target of our anger and ourselves, anger can also distort and destroy social relationships. Love brings people together; anger, a distorted form of self-love, pushes people apart. A gang member shoots a member of a rival gang because "He didn't show me no respect." The second gang wants revenge and shoots a member of the first gang, and the process goes on destroying the peace and security of a neighborhood or an entire city.

The divisions created by anger can be long-lasting. The parents of six children died leaving about $300,000 to be divided evenly among them. Two of the boys had borrowed money from their parents that they had never repaid. The other four thought that the debt should be deducted from the two brothers' shares. When the two said that the parents had never intended for them to repay, tempers flared. No solution was reached and for twenty years the four never talked with the other two. Anger ruined that family's harmony.

Civil strife; lack of cooperation between groups such as management and labor; suspicions between racial, religious or ethnic communities—all can be caused by anger at past injustices even though the present generation is trying to act in a fair and just manner.

'I Choose to Be Angry!'

Our actions can often provide a clue that we are angry. Some warning blip on our threat screen causes us to be sullen, to give someone the cold shoulder, to blow our top, to give vent to sarcasm or to make a sharp critical remark. Often we do not want to claim that anger. We tend to blame the actions or words of others when we feel annoyed, peeved, miffed, upset, agitated, irked or riled up.

After a meeting one man asked his coworker, "Were you angry at me?" The coworker said, "No. Why do you think I was angry?" The first explained how the coworker had turned his eyes away whenever he spoke in the meeting. The coworker paused and finally said, "Maybe you are right. I was angry because of the way you cut off the fellow from finance who was talking. I thought ignoring what he had to say was most impolite and unkind."

Or our anger can get confused with other feelings: being used, put down, ignored or rejected. Depression may be a sign of anger that is turned inward instead of being dealt with in a positive way. And righteous indignation may be a cloak hiding angry vengeance rather than a thirst for justice.

What most people do not realize is that there is nothing another person can do to *make us* angry. When we perceive—whether rightly or wrongly—that some aspect of our personhood is under attack, *we decide* whether to become angry. The same words spoken to two different people will produce anger in one but not in the other.

In a real sense *we choose to be angry*. Not every choice is a conscious one. Some may come from force of habit. But we choose to allow that habit of anger to continue if we fail to examine and deal with the distorted image of ourself that keeps it operating.

An important help in taking responsibility for one's anger is identifying the spot in our psyche that is hurting, the button that is being pushed to signal threat. Maybe it is an inflated self-importance, a need to be in control, a desire to gather and hold possessions, a yearning for physical pleasure.

Finding this tender spot may not be easy. It helps, however, to keep an inventory of the times during a day when we feel upset or in other ways detect the stirrings of anger. We can ask: Why did I get angry when that car cut me off, or when the lady with the shopping cart full of groceries got into express checkout? What in me was threatened by those actions? We can ask these kinds of questions about whatever another says or does that upsets us: Why do I feel at least a tinge of anger when I hear a sexist remark, or fail to persuade another during a political discussion, or see pictures of starving children on the news? The answers to such questions will, in time, reveal what is out of kilter in the way we assess the threat in people and situations and decide to respond.

Counting to Ten

Advice abounds on how to deal with situations that activate the virus of anger. Some say, "Forget it," as if a person who is hurt can easily do that. Others say, "Anger is wrong. Don't get angry," as if we have absolute control over our feelings.

Still others caution, "Count to ten before speaking or acting," and that is pretty good advice. Taking that deep breath gives us a moment to consider whether the fight or flight reaction we are about to take is really in our own best interests or that of others. But, sadly, this advice is seldom followed.

In recent years books and courses on how to deal with anger have proliferated. Some counsel vigorous physical activity because of the strong bodily element in our anger. Adrenaline is being pumped into the blood stream, muscles are tightening ready for action. Physical activity brings the body back to a more normal balance and so lessens the impact of our anger.

Other writers counsel assertiveness, but there is a very thin line between assertion and aggression. Aggression usually takes the form of a verbal attack on the other. In those situations when it is prudent and helpful to express the fact that we are angry and are asserting our rights, it should be done with kindness and concern. I think of the people at airline check-in counters who are so often the brunt of angry attacks when a flight is canceled or someone gets bumped by overbooking.

Reason says, "Be gentle in your disagreements while holding on to your convictions." When making an assertion it is important to use first-person pronouns. For example: "I feel angry because teasing hurts and brings up bad memories of the past." This statement reports and owns the anger.

But look at this statement in contrast: "You make me angry when you tease me." It attempts to shift the blame to the other person.

Some instructors say, "Let it all hang out." They suggest shouting, screaming and expressing your anger. This may release tension, but what do we gain by placing the blame on others, or injuring their feelings, or engendering further bitterness and recriminations?

Someone who comes from a home where blow-ups are frequent but quickly forgotten may not realize that such expressions of anger can frighten, intimidate or alienate a person with a different upbringing. An ardent feminist once verbally attacked a celebrant after Sunday Mass as an insensitive male chauvinist who had insulted all the women in the congregation because he had not eliminated all sexist language in the Mass prayers. No doubt *she* felt better, but the priest was now filled with anger because he felt unfairly attacked. He had changed a great deal of the language and believed he had good reasons for not changing the rest.

The anger virus hides deep in the soul and is almost impossible to eliminate entirely. The best we can do is control it. As with any infection it is important to catch it as soon as possible.

With most people the first sign of an onslaught of anger is *physical*. The throat constricts, the stomach tightens or the blood pressure rises. This is the time to take the antibiotics of reason and reflection. Reason is needed to step in and say, "Stop and look at this situation *before* acting. Is there a real threat to my well-being or only a projection of my fears? Is the other person really vicious or merely insensitive? Am I being *hyper*sensitive?"

If the threat proves real, reason must ask further questions: "Was it intended?" If unintended, we can choose to ignore it. If intended, our reason must reach beyond violence for tools to deal with the threat. Two of these are a forgiving smile and an understanding heart. These—not tit for tat—are the signs of those who are blessed as merciful and who will receive mercy (see Matthew 5:7).

In many situations reason has little chance to raise its voice between the first physical warnings that we feel threatened and the welling up within us of uncontrolled angry impulses. Reason has to struggle to be heard while it is trying to contain the fever. But whether reason succeeds or fails, we must look back afterward to identify the occasion for the anger and how we responded to it. This is a helpful practice, particularly if we then try to imagine a more positive and helpful way to handle a similar future situation.

Exercises in imagination are important because most people have only one more or less set way of responding when they feel threatened. Frequently this can be traced back to our basic temperament or to a pattern established in early childhood. It may not be appropriate in every situation in later life.

There is no one best way to tame anger. We need an arsenal of responses. These can only be developed as we recognize how we usually react and then imagine and reflect on other reactions that might be more beneficial. For example: "I could have said this instead of what I did say. Then I could have left the room till I cooled down. And, later, I could have calmly told the person how I felt."

As we think of different ways to respond in future situations it is helpful to picture the situation in detail, hearing the words, replaying the actions, feeling the emotions. Then we can imagine ourself responding in a more positive manner. The hope is that the next time the alarm bell goes off, this alternative way of responding will come to mind so we can handle our anger in a more reasonable and peaceful way.

Solomon Schimmel suggests keeping an anger diary (*The Seven Deadly Sins*, pages 103-104). In it we record daily answers to the following questions about specific incidents that provoked us to anger:

- Could I have avoided the provocations?

- Was my response justified?
- Was my response too intense? Did it accomplish its goal?
- What unfortunate side effects did my response have?
- What alternative response could I have made?
- Would I react otherwise if the incident were repeated?
- Am I to be blamed or praised for my behavior?

The remedy for the virus of anger suggested by all spiritual writers is to cultivate the opposite virtues. Just as there are many words in the English language to describe degrees of anger, so there are many words to describe the virtues that help one tame anger: Forbearance, humility, patience, compassion, empathy, joy, humor and peace are but a few.

The two virtues directly opposed to anger are meekness and clemency (mercy). It is impossible in a given situation to be both meek and angry, both merciful and angry.

Meekness, unfortunately, has a bad name. It conjures up a picture of a wishy-washy, spineless pushover. But meekness in fact requires great strength. It means that one endures injury with patience and without resentment. The "with patience" part of meekness may, in fact, be easier to practice than the "without resentment" part. But together they are the steel rods in the spine of the meek person.

Meekness restrains anger within the bounds of reason. The meek person is truly master of himself or herself. Walter Farrell describes the meek man as "a fearless rider on a wild steed which he has so tamed that it swerves to his lightest touch" (*Companion to the Summa*, vol. 3, page 456).

Surely this is what Jesus had in mind when he said, "Blessed are the meek, for they will inherit the earth" (Matthew 5:5). He would hardly promise the kingdom to the spineless, the wishy-washy.

The virtue of clemency moves us beyond the narrow justice of "an eye for an eye and a tooth for a tooth." It moderates the desire for revenge and punishment with forgiveness and an understanding of the motives and weaknesses of others.

41

This, too, is a habit found only in the strong. It does not condone what the other has done. It sees the action, the inflicted injury, for what it was, but it mercifully seeks the conversion and redemption of the person rather than punishment for its own sake.

Memory, too, can be a big help in taming anger. It helps reason by bringing to mind the pain caused by past outbursts of anger as well as the peace and understanding in other situations when meekness and the other virtues turned off the red alert.

Memory can also summon help by remembering wise words such as those of the Roman philosopher Seneca, who said it is better to accept human frailty in a spirit of forgiveness and understanding than to harbor anger and punish offenders out of a spirit of hatred. It can also recall the words of Jesus:

- "But I say to you that if you are angry with a brother or sister, you will be liable to judgment" (Matthew 5:22).

- "But if anyone strikes you on the right cheek, turn the other also" (5:39).

- "[L]ove your enemies and pray for those who persecute you" (5:44).

- "[F]orgive us our debts,/as we also have forgiven our debtors" (6:12).

If we reflect on these wise words in our calmer moments, memory will see that they pop into our head when the alarm bell goes off, our anger is blazing red hot and we are counting to ten.

A final help in taming anger is to meditate on and pray over the way Jesus handled unjust attacks—even physical violence. He never attributed bad motives to anyone except the hypocrites. He saw the good in people. On the cross he forgave his killers because they did not realize what they were doing. Jesus was so secure in knowing he was loved by God that nothing others said or did to him could trigger angry reactions that he could not control.

Anger is second only to pride in the harm and suffering it causes in our lives and in our world. Anger warns, "You are being attacked! Defend yourself! Get vengeance!"

But reason and grace say, "Stop and think! Count to ten! Identify why you are angry. Take ownership of your anger! Look for kind and just ways to deal with the perceived threat."

For Reflection

1. *Dante's* Divine Comedy *pictures the angry man in purgatory unable to see anything around him because he is surrounded by clouds of smoke from the fire burning within him. What does this image suggest about the effects of anger in our lives?*

2. *What are the things that cause you or someone you know to get angry when you are driving? Why do they trigger anger?*

3. *What is the button—the tender spot in your pysche—that is pushed when you feel anger rising in you?*

4. *Do you think anger is sometimes justified? If so, what virtues do you think have to be practiced in conjunction with this anger?*

5. *What do you find helpful in taming your anger?*

Prayer

LORD, when my button is pushed and I feel angry, help me realize that I need to forgive just as I have been unconditionally forgiven by you.

CHAPTER FIVE

Greed

The phone rang and Tom, the voice of some brokerage house, wanted to know if I would like to make 12 to 14 percent on an investment. I said, "No."

Surprised, Tom asked, "Why not?"

"I have enough income for my needs," I said.

Tom's voice went up a notch or two: "You mean you don't want to make more money?"

"I don't."

With a trace of surprise and anger, Tom responded, "I've never talked to anyone who didn't want to make more money." And then he hung up.

I did not refuse Tom's offer because I am totally detached from worldly possessions or totally unconcerned about my financial future. But I did refuse Tom's appeal to my greed because I did not want the bother of worrying about the safety of my investment or about what I would do with the interest.

Tom should have been talking instead to the musician I once saw interviewed on MTV. When he first began to play, he said, he just wanted to make a million dollars and retire. He soon realized, however, that he wouldn't stop there. When he had that million he would want a second million and then a third. He had already learned the lesson that money can be a never-ending, all-consuming pursuit.

Going Too Far to Get and to Keep

Ancient writers call the inordinate desire to pile up wealth and possessions by different names—greed, covetousness, avarice. Its sinfulness and malice lies in going too far to acquire possessions and too far to keep them. It spawns a host of other sins—cheating, lying, perjury, violence. It leads to betrayal of friends, hard-heartedness, indifference to the plight of the poor and needy and blindness to the reality of an afterlife.

People need a certain amount of material goods and money to live a decent human life and to provide for the future. The question is: When does the legitimate desire to meet present needs become immoderate and exceed reasonable limits? When is the desire for a larger house, a better car, a more exotic vacation inordinate? When does setting aside money for one's future security exceed reasonable limits and become an exercise in hoarding for the sake of hoarding?

These questions cannot be easily answered. People in different social positions will have differing needs.

Everyone certainly needs at least one pair of shoes. Most of us even need several pairs of shoes for different occasions. And people who make frequent public appearances as part of their job or a spouse's job will certainly need more shoes than a postal clerk who wears a uniform to work every day. But no one, including Imelda Marcos as first lady of the Philippines, needs 6,000 pairs of shoes to be well-dressed.

It is easy to see a street person's desire for enough money to get a meal and rent a room as reasonable. Likewise, the search for a better-paying job by a person only one paycheck away from eviction is well within the bounds of reason.

But what about the man I met on a plane on his way to the East Coast for a new job that would pay him over $100,000 a year. That was 35 percent more than he had been earning, he explained. His wife had refused to move with him, so he had to make a choice between her and the money. He was choosing the money.

Certainly there seems to be something inordinate about this man's desire for a bigger paycheck. Contrast this with the choices many others make every day to forego promotions and higher salaries in order to maintain proximity to family and friends. They decide to make do with less.

But what is reasonable or unreasonable about money and possessions is not always so clear. Sometimes two TVs help keep peace in a family, but does a family need a TV in every room? What about people who love to shop? Are they being thrifty in searching for the best bargains for their families, or are they greedy in seeking out bargains even though they do not need the items?

Credit cards can feed the virus of greed. An elderly lady filled her home with lamps, jewelry and pictures she did not need and could not use because she saw them on the shopping channel—and could easily purchase them over the phone with her major credit card.

A young man who had been raised in a family of modest means received several credit cards in the mail. He bought all the things he ever wanted—a shotgun, a camera, skis, a boat and all sorts of household appliances. Soon he was having difficulty paying the interest on the cards and had to go to his father for help. Living beyond one's means is probably one of the most easily recognized signs that greed is at work in one's life.

In the United States, in spite of the millions of people living below the poverty line, most people are not needy. Their struggle is not to meet basic needs but to deal with the virus of greed in a society based on the premise that everyone, no matter how much he or she already has, needs more. Not every desire to make more money or to improve one's standard of living is a sign of greed, but it is extremely difficult for most of us to draw the fine line between covetousness and moderation.

Henry Fairlie in *The Seven Deadly Sins Today* detects the virus of greed at work in one of America's most basic institutions—the large shopping mall. He says:

> The most important fact about our shopping malls, as distinct from the ordinary shopping center where we go for our groceries, is that we do not need most of what they sell, not even for our pleasure or

entertainment, not really even for a sensation of luxury. Little in them is essential to our survival, our work, or our play, and the same is true of the boutiques that multiply on our streets.... Our appetites are stimulated so that the produce will be consumed, and thus we are incited to possess for the sake of possessing. We "must have that," when we see it, even though we do not need it. We buy more clothes than we need,...more furniture than we need, more bric-a-brac than we need, more objets d'art than we need, more cookbooks than we need,...and even more gifts for our friends than they need.

The need to acquire, to have as much or more than others, to show by what we own that we have succeeded—this is simply taken for granted in our society. Few question it. This attitude gets expressed and justified in many slogans:

- "You deserve it; you've worked hard."

- "More is better."

- "The new is better than the old."

- "If you can afford it, get it."

- "If you have it, flaunt it."

And people will say that if you do not desire to have more things, you have no ambition, that you have given up on life.

Our society does not encourage the kind of questions that would help us sort out what is reasonable and moderate from what is inordinate. We need to ask questions like:

- Do I really need this?

- Will the old serve as well as the new?

- How can I get along with less rather than more so I am better able to help others?

I met a young man with a wife and two children on vacation, and he asked to talk confidentially about a serious problem. I expected a tale of marital woes, but his problem was deciding how to draw that fine line between a reasonable standard of living and one that seemed inordinate to him.

His company was successful, he said, but he did not like some of what that entailed. He and his partners had built the business from scratch. Now his partners were after him to move to the suburbs as they had done "for the sake of the business." But he liked the working-class section of the city in which he lived. They were also pushing him to join an expensive golf club in the area "for the sake of the business." He did not play golf nor did he want his children associating with the set who gathered at the pool and went to expensive prep schools. His partners urged him to get rid of his four-year-old station wagon and buy a car more befitting an executive of a successful company.

He did not know what to do. He shrewdly foresaw that more and more demands would be made to "improve" the image of the company by "upgrading" his standard of living. He also foresaw that if he did all the things his partners suggested, he would be forced to be more and more concerned about making enough money to pay for the cars, houses and clubs he did not particularly want. He was afraid that making money might become the focus of his life.

I wish I knew how he solved his problem. He rightly saw that turning luxuries into necessities might easily change his priorities, that making money instead of being with his growing children might become the center of his activities. He was wrestling with the siren call of greed.

One cannot label as greedy all people who make large amounts of money. Some people just love what they do and keep on working even when they no longer need the money. Others just happen to have talents that are excessively compensated in our free-market economy.

Greed lies not in the amount one has but in *the desire to accumulate more* even when one already has what is sufficient and reasonable. It flourishes when we constantly strive to acquire all that we want rather than being satisfied with what we need.

The virus of greed is fostered early in life by parents who

give children everything they want. Does a child who can be happy playing with an empty box or dressing in old clothes need a room full of toys? What does the overabundance of toys, and especially of expensive ones, teach a child about moderation and frugality?

Reader's Digest recently ran a story about a little girl out shopping with her father. She asked him to buy a doll she saw in a window. He saw this request as a wonderful opportunity to teach his daughter the difference between need and want. So he explained that although she *wanted* another doll she did not *need* it; she already had three or four at home. Her reply captured the true American spirit: "But Daddy, when I want something, I need it." Greed had already wrapped insidious tentacles around her young heart.

Besides merely wanting *to accumulate more*, greed and avarice can also involve the desire *to hang on to whatever we have*. Scrooge huddled over his account books and Silas Marner counting his gold coins are personifications of the miser, the one whose sole concern is to hold on to his money. But people can be miserly about things other than money.

The art collector who buys a great masterpiece and then hangs it where only he can enjoy it is as miserly as Scrooge. People can also be miserly with their time—refusing to say yes when another requests it or needs it. When asked to volunteer time, they always come up with an excuse. It's not because they are really too busy, but they do not want to give up any of their precious time. Some people may be generous with their money (and even make a large monetary contribution), but they are misers with their time.

What causes one to be greedy or miserly? There are many answers: a lack of necessities in one's younger life, the desire to keep up with the Joneses, the extravagant demands of a spouse or other family members, the lure of advertising, the need for a sense of security and the permanence of things. But some people who appear greedy may, in fact, be more motivated by the need to bolster their self-confidence and self-esteem. Wearing a $15,000 Rolex or driving a Jaguar makes them feel better about themselves.

All of the capital sins are perversions of love and drive out genuine love. Greed is no exception. Avaricious actions build walls between those seeking to get more and those trying to hang onto all they have. The disputes between owners and players of sports teams is a good example of each side trying to get all they can from the game.

Many disputes between labor and management come down to the same thing. Management seeks to maximize profits and returns for the stockholders; labor tries to get a bigger piece of the pie for themselves. They view each other as adversaries to be overcome instead of as partners working for the common good. An inordinate desire for money on both sides destroys trust and breeds mistrust.

Every time there is a scandal about a political figure using public office for personal gain, voters lose respect for the system. Investors do not know whom to trust because financial pages carry stories every week of another con game that bilked people out of their life savings, of corporate takeovers that cost people their jobs, of the unreasonable use of other people's money as in the savings and loan debacles.

Greed also distorts the way we look at others. Sweatshop operators, con artists, modern-day robber barons—all look at people as less than human. They are seen merely as means for improving the bottom line.

Greed has had tremendously destructive effects on society. Many wars have been driven by greed. Before the modern age the quickest way for one nation or city-state to increase its wealth was to take the wealth and property of another.

Desire to make money without regard for social consequences lies behind much of the depletion of natural resources in our own country and around the world. Areas of the ocean are fished out. Virgin forests are cut bare and erosion destroys the soil. Mining companies leave behind heaps of rock and chemicals to poison the soil and streams.

Today's battles over environmental protection laws are often infected with the virus of greed. Care and moderation in the use of natural resources in order to conserve them for future generations costs money and means less profit today.

Avarice also hurts the greedy person. Over-concern about acquiring money leaves little time to be concerned about growing in the love of God and in service to one's neighbor. Much of the joy and freedom in life is lost if one is constantly penny-pinching or evaluating every situation in terms of how it can be turned to one's monetary advantage. It causes one to be suspicious and always worried that one is being cheated or robbed.

'If I Want It, I Need It!'

Greed is identified by whether our desire to acquire or hold onto things is moderate and reasonable or inordinate and therefore unreasonable. Drawing the line between moderation and greed is made difficult by the fact that every increase in what we have leads to a higher standard for judging what is reasonable and what is inordinate. Things we would have considered luxuries at one time become necessities. Most people today need an automobile. But what is a *reasonable* car? A Geo? A Toyota? A Lincoln Continental? A Mercedes?

My first car years ago was a two-door, stick-shift, stripped-down, bottom-of-the-line Ford. It was clearly basic transportation. Four years later an automatic transmission did not seem too great a luxury. A radio came with the next car. In time the summer heat seemed to make air conditioning a necessity. I never chose electric windows and door locks, but they were standard on one of my recent cars. All these accessories now seem perfectly reasonable when I go looking for a new car.

I have frequently asked myself whether my desire to have these accessories on my car is inordinate. When I discussed my dilemma with a friend, he gave me a business man's insight into my problem. He suggested that I consider what would happen to the American economy if the only car people bought was a version of Henry Ford's black Model T—and if they drove it until it literally fell apart. He outlined all the people who would not have a means of livelihood. He spoke glowingly of the virtue of competition that results in

52

new and improved products that create wants that, in time, become needs.

The economic imperatives of our industrial, technological and global society do make it much more difficult to identify greed. Things do have to be produced and purchased in order to provide work for the ninety-eight percent of the people in this country who do not live by farming.

Naming and claiming greed is made even more difficult, however, because we tend to give other names to our unreasonable and immoderate desire to acquire wealth. We call it "good business," a "reasonable return on our investment," "deserved compensation," "growing the economy," "providing for our future." All of these can, of course, be good reasons for accumulating money.

It is impossible to set a dollar figure on what amount of money is moderate when we are looking at our present and future needs. But when a large corporation is bought out, does the CEO who has been making well over a million dollars a year need a $5- or $10-million-dollar golden parachute at the same time that several thousand people lose their jobs?

The most ingenious excuse I have ever heard for building up one's wealth is this: "Where would the Church be if some people did not have big bucks to contribute to the building funds?"

Most people do not have the problem of making and hoarding "big bucks," but they may still show signs of greed. They can be stingy in sharing what they do have with the poor. They may spend so much time bargain-hunting for the simplest purchases that they have no time to volunteer for worthwhile community projects. Or they may so incessantly talk about the price of everything—cars, shoes, houses, groceries—that it drives other topics from conversation and from their own consciousness.

Throwing money away foolishly, failing to make reasonable provision for the future, giving all one's possessions away, going on welfare, moving to skid row— none of these behaviors is a virtuous counter to greed. And each of these may, in a perverse way, actually be a form of greed at work.

Greed may also lurk in the way we use the money we have—by spending it only on ourselves or to meet the needs of our own family. It can influence our thoughts and attitudes about caring for the poor—by making us unreasonably opposed to any increase in taxes. It can even be present if we deprive ourselves of something we need, such as medical care, in order to save money. Perhaps the sneaky virus of greed shows up just as frequently in *how we use and share what we have*, as in our striving to acquire more.

Finding the meaning of moderation for oneself is never easy. But there is a balance somewhere for each of us. Before we can find that balance, however, we need to look at our attitudes about the importance of material things and at our habits of acquiring and holding on to them—and sharing them with others.

Being Generous in Small Things

The first step in taming greed is acknowledging that the virus does exist in us and that it can show itself in small as well as in colossal ways. We all—those with vows of poverty as well as those with signifcant stock portfolios—have to examine what we do to get the things we want and how we feel about holding on to what we have. In a religious community in which all things are held in common, saying "That is *my* pen!" can be as sure an indicator of greed as the efforts of a Wall Street broker to parlay his three billion dollars into four.

Taming greed is very much like losing weight. We do it a little at a time by practicing the opposite virtue of liberality, or generosity, in little things. Then when a big temptation to be greedy comes along, it will not be too hard to resist.

I know a man who reads a lot. When he finishes a book, he immediately gives it away because he does not want to be weighed down by possessions. He places people above riches or possessions, and he is willing to share. His generosity in giving away books is an antidote to greed.

Sometimes liberality can go a bit too far. A most generous priest was known for his willingness to loan his car to anyone who needed it. In fact, when his car was out on loan, he would hand out the keys to the pastor's car or to the car of another priest in the house—without their consent. Such "generosity" with the possessions of others is in conflict with justice. But generosity rightly exercised makes life easier for people in need and greases the wheels of social relationships.

Taming avarice also requires examining our own desires—beginning with the seemingly inconsequential: a desire for a more comfortable chair, a nicer suit, another dress. We need to ask:

- Do I really need this?
- Why do I want more of this or that?
- Can my energies and resources be put to better use in some other way?
- Is it necessary for me to keep up with the latest fashions or fads?
- Can I get along just as well with a little less and give a little more to those who really need it?

Often we need the help and advice of a spiritual director to detect the signs of greed in our lives and to determine whether a desire is reasonable or not. A writer comfortable with an electric typewriter mulled over whether buying a computer was justified. Her spiritual director asked whether it would aid in her work. She listed three or four ways it would. The director advised her to buy it because her work was important. The director helped her see her desire as reasonable and moderate.

Regularly questioning whether our desire to buy something new or better is reasonable and moderate will help keep us conscious of the sneaky ways society promotes greed and of the reality of this capital sin in our lives.

For Reflection

1. What are some concrete examples of how our society promotes and justifies greed?

2. Give some examples of people you know who seem inordinately attached to things? Can you cite examples in your own life?

3. Reflecting on how the opposite virtue is present in our life can often help in taming the capital sin. How generous are you?

   - Do you freely and without second thought give money to good causes and to people in need?

   - Do you freely loan out your possessions?

   - How do you feel about losing a possession through theft or fire—or about being cheated out of money?

4. How do you decide what is moderate and reasonable when you would like to have a new car, new clothes, a vacation, an evening out and so on?

Prayer

LORD, you have freely given me all the gifts I have. Help me share them just as freely with others—especially those who have less than I. And deliver me from all inordinate attachments to money or possessions.

▼▼▼▼▼▼▼▼▼▼▼▼▼
Gluttony
▲▲▲▲▲▲▲▲▲▲▲▲▲

I sat with the menu, debating whether to have a hamburger with fries or a chicken salad. A little voice seemed to say, "Don't worry about the cholesterol today; 290 isn't too bad and you are only 20 pounds overweight." Gluttony was making its devilish voice heard.

My debate was interrupted as three people sat down at the next table. Just a few more pounds and each of them could have qualified as a sumo wrestler. Each started with a gigantic plate of french-fried onion rings. Then came the pastrami sandwiches piled so high they severely challenged the welcoming mouths. The appetizers and sandwiches were accompanied by large Cokes and followed by cheesecake.

Meanwhile, I did not completely resist gluttony's temptation. My compromise was to order a hamburger *without* the fries.

At the end of lunch (theirs and mine), another little voice seemed to say to me, "See what happens if you allow your food to begin to eat you."

What's Eating (or Drinking) You?

Food and drink serve a variety of purposes. They do not merely provide fuel to keep the body alive; they also contribute to good health.

They please not only our palates but our other senses as well. We find real pleasure in the smoothness of rich ice cream and in the crunch of crisp celery sticks. An elderly woman at whose house I have eaten would discreetly inquire about my preference of vegetables because she wanted to arrange the plate with a variety of textures and colors in order to make it more pleasing to the eye.

In addition to sensual pleasure, a good meal or a favorite food can provide emotional comfort after a trying day. And eating and drinking are also meant to promote companionship. Very few people enjoy eating alone. The family dinner, the business luncheon, coffee and dessert at a friend's house, even a beer with friends at the corner bar are more than ways to nourish the body. They also satisfy our need to be with others.

Like all other God-given gifts, however, we can put too much or too little emphasis on food or drink. In doing so we pervert the end for which they were created, and we allow them to become destructive of companionship, of pleasure and of life itself.

The way those three people at the next table in the deli went at their onion rings and pastrami personified, for me, the destructive effects of gluttony. Certainly the weight they carried and the fats they consumed were not good for their health. Yet they showed little enjoyment in what they were eating—shoveling it in without savoring its flavor or noticing its texture. Worst of all, they hardly spoke a word to one another during the whole meal. They concentrated on the food and ignored the people with whom they were sharing it. Eating without talking and gobbling food that fast is destructive of the pleasure and companionship that food and drink are meant to provide along with the nourishment.

We use the word *glutton* in a variety of ways. It can mean one who has a large capacity for accepting or enduring something. We say of a boxer, "He was a glutton for punishment," meaning that he took a beating in the ring. It also means one who eats or drinks in a greedy or voracious manner. Years ago Orson Welles vividly portrayed Falstaff as a pot-bellied glutton chewing on an entire chicken, tossing the bones over his shoulder and quaffing pints of ale.

As a capital sin, gluttony is the inclination to an inordinate desire for food or drink. This inclination may lead to excessive eating or drinking. The habitual immoderate consumption of food or drink gives rise to attitudes and behaviors that make food and/or drink the center of one's life. We call these habits "addictions."

But overconcern about food can also lead to the irrational refusal to eat or drink enough. This is the situation with people suffering from anorexia.

It is difficult to draw the line between a reasonable and unreasonable desire for food and drink or between moderate and immoderate enjoyment of them. Gross forms of gluttony are not difficult to identify: in the person who always has to have a drink in hand, or in someone who is constantly eating. It is not so easy to recognize in people who are only twenty or thirty pounds overweight or who drink too much only now and then.

Modern research has identified physical and psychological reasons other than the mere enjoyment of food or drink that can cause one to be immoderate in eating or drinking. Psychological needs or personal problems as well as our genetic makeup can be at the root of an inordinate use of food or drink. Irrespective of the cause, however, eating and drinking habits that harm one's health or relationships are unreasonable and a sign of the virus of gluttony.

Most of us do not have a problem with gluttony at a serious level. Yet the virus of gluttony may still be operating in a sneaky way in our lives. If our mothers enrolled us in the clean plate club and we've remained faithful members ever since, we are most likely eating more than is good for us a good part of the time. A diet heavy in chips, hot dogs, soft drinks and candy bars may not seem unreasonable when we are young, but this type of diet certainly is not healthy over a lifetime. It is immoderate.

We do not, of course, have to restrict our intake of food or drink to that which is absolutely necessary to sustain life. Eating more than the bare minimum because one enjoys it, because it relieves the tension of the moment, because it fosters friendship and hospitality can all be good. Centuries ago Saint Augustine asked, "Who is it, Lord, who does not eat a little more than is necessary?"

The important question is this: When does one's "a little more than is necessary" push the boundaries of reason and moderation? There are no hard and fast guidelines aside from one obvious limit: Drinking or eating oneself into a stupor is clearly unreasonable.

Beyond that, what is reasonable for one person may not be for another. It may be reasonable, for example, for a football player to put away two steaks and several baked potatoes after a hard game. It certainly is not reasonable for a couch potato to do the same.

The abundance and variety of food available at all times in our supermarkets and restaurants can cater in subtle ways to gluttony. Any trip to such establishments can be a temptation to consume more than is reasonable or moderate. On the other hand, that same variety and abundance can temper gluttony. If melons or strawberries are available all year—not just for the few weeks of a local season—there is less temptation to gorge on them now.

Modern methods of growing and preserving food, which depend on pesticides and chemical additives, cause questions about moderation and reasonableness to be raised in a new context. Some think the consumption of such foods is unhealthy and therefore unreasonable. Others think the nutritional value and pleasure of these foods justifies the small risk involved in eating them *in moderation*.

What are some less serious and less obvious habits that indicate that gluttony is at work? Isn't it a sign that a person is unreasonably concerned about food if, at the end of each meal, he or she begins immediately to think about what will be served at the next meal? (It is reasonable, of course, to spend time and thought on a meal one is preparing for guests.)

What about the habit of constantly sampling or nibbling food even when one is not hungry? Dagwood, a humorous character in the comics, always has his fingers on the appetizers and dishes his wife Blondie, a caterer, has prepared. He is a comic character precisely because we recognize in his actions things we do ourselves that we sense are not always reasonable. Might not the habit of being the first at the appetizer tray and the first at the table indicate that the desire to enjoy food is not fully under our control? Some dietitians advocate eating small amounts of food every few hours instead of two or three large meals in order to keep food in the stomach and avoid that hungry feeling that causes us to eat more food than we need. But this does not mean it is reasonable to snack constantly *and* still eat three regular meals.

What about fussy or finicky eaters who have all sorts of likes and dislikes unrelated to health? The potential sin here does not have to do with what foods a person eats or doesn't eat but with the overconcern about enjoying whatever food is put on one's plate.

What about those health-food faddists who are always talking about the unhealthy properties of red meat, salt, sugar, preservatives and so on? They put others off by telling them what to eat and what not to eat, and they bore them with incessant talk about the latest findings about this or that food. Their focus on food is unreasonable because, in a perverse way, it destroys their ability to enjoy the food served at an ordinary meal. It also destroys the enjoyment of others! Such faddists cause embarrassment and confusion for a host when they come to dinner with their list of things they do not eat or cannot eat. (Of course it is perfectly reasonable to alert a host to serious food allergies.)

In *The Screwtape Letters*, C. S. Lewis has the older, more clever devil advise the young apprentice devil about how to tempt a woman. He encourages her to be very fussy about her toast. It is too dark. The butter is not right. She only wants one piece without the crust, and so on. All the time she is talking about being abstemious but, in reality, food is the center of her life and is alienating her from the people who have to serve her.

We may ask whether people preoccupied with gaining or losing a few pounds for the sake of appearance are not hosts to the virus of gluttony. These people often go on crash diets that can injure their health. They also bore others with incessant talk about their need to diet and their latest diet plan. We may ask the same question about the food and wine connoisseurs who must always eat in the very best restaurants or drink the very best wines, who are always seeking exotic and unusual cuisines. It does seem there is a certain lack of moderation in such habits.

A great many social events are planned around eating and drinking. It is a compliment to the guests if the host or hostess plans and prepares tasty food and drink. But if they are more concerned about the food than the guests, and if they focus all conversation on the food, there may well be an element of gluttony in their entertaining.

Overconcern about what one is eating or drinking can give birth to other types of sins such as uncharitableness or unkindness. Showing irritation with the server in a restaurant when the meat or vegetables are not done to one's taste could well be a sign of gluttony. Such a person is upset because his or her eating pleasure has been diminished even though the food will certainly nourish the body.

This immoderate concern can also defeat the social or friendship purpose of food and drink. I do not enjoy dining with fussy eaters who find fault with something—or everything—at any meal. Their complaints, beside spoiling my meal, often make the life of the cook miserable. Fastidiousness with food or drink may not be wrong in itself, but it certainly becomes wrong if it causes others embarrassment or unnecessary pain.

I do not like mushy pasta. But if I complain in an unkind way to the waiter or cook, if I cause a scene when it is served, or if I avoid a friend's invitation to dinner because his spaghetti is always soggy, a subtle form of gluttony is causing me to violate charity. The pasta, instead of bringing me closer to the people who prepare it and serve it and want to eat it with me, erects a barrier of inconsiderateness between us.

'My Food Is Eating Me!'

Naming and claiming our habits of drinking or eating as signs of gluttony is not easy. Hard and fast norms are few. Is the habit of downing a drink in one or two swallows while others slowly sip and enjoy theirs a small indication of gluttony? Is rushing to the table and gobbling our food a sign that the virus is at work in us? What about filling up on appetizers just because they are there and the meal has not been served? Are the martinis before lunch or the de rigueur cocktails before dinner indications that alcohol is becoming a habit I cannot easily control? Taking responsibility for these habits often is much harder because society gives us so many reasons or excuses for them.

I imagine that if someone spoke to those three incipient sumo wrestlers next to me in the deli and suggested they were gluttons, they would laugh it off. At best they might admit to an eating disorder caused by emotional starvation or abuse as children. They might even blame their genes or the fact that they were fed an early diet too heavy in starches.

One or all of these reasons may be true, but reasons such as these do not take away our responsibility to name our actions honestly. Those folks in the deli were abusing a God-given gift and behaving in a way destructive of health and of their relationship to one another.

It is humiliating but rather easy to acknowledge that *at times* we have eaten or drunk to an excess. It is not easy to admit that one's eating or drinking *habits* are immoderate and therefore irrational, gluttonous. Instead of taking responsibility for them people deny or excuse themselves.

The alcoholic who refuses to do something about his drinking is a prime example of a person in denial. Many people who are addicted to excessive eating or drinking blame their actions on a glandular disorder or on genetic inheritance. In doing so they refuse to take responsibility for their actions. Other people refuse to claim the sin of gluttony because they use immoderate amounts of food or drink as a way of dealing with stress or as compensation for the emotional starvation or abuse they suffer.

Parents often use food as a reward for children. "If you clean your plate, you can have ice cream." But using food to reward oneself for doing something good or healthy can be unreasonable and serve as an excuse to escape responsibility. A man who was struggling to follow the diet given him by his doctor would be careful to eat poached fish and salads without dressing. Then he would reward himself with an ice-cream dessert because he "deserved it" for being so good.

One or all of these excuses or reasons for overindulging may be operating in a particular case and diminish a person's moral culpability. But no matter how deeply ingrained the habit is, or the cause of it, a person still has the responsibility to do something about it.

Seeking Support and Saying No

Taming gluttony is much easier said than done. To realize how difficult it is we merely have to think of the many diets we have begun, or the times we have tried to give up smoking or drinking. Lent comes and we decide to give up sweets for forty days. How often do we last an entire week?

Keeping the virus of gluttony in check requires the old-fashioned virtues of temperance and self-denial. Both of these are out of style in our modern society which places such great value on getting all you can out of life and getting it now.

For these virtues to kick in and develop, a strong motive is often needed. A health problem or some realization of the other harms done by smoking, drinking or taking drugs can motivate a change in a person's habits of overindulging. Even less powerful motives—the feeling of being uncomfortable with our weight, the embarrassing effects of too many glasses of wine at dinner, the desire to get in better shape—can cause us to resolve to go on a diet or to correct eating or drinking habits.

All of us know that these resolutions are usually useless unless the will to change is more than a mere wish to do so. For twenty-five years the doctor has told me to lose weight. I have always agreed with him and have promised to diet. But somehow or other I have always found good reason for breaking my resolution "just this one time." It is difficult to control what is set before me because I frequently travel or go out to dinner. I find it hard to leave some of the food on the plate or to refuse one little piece of cake. My long ingrained habits of eating always overwhelm my most sincere desires.

Very often the support of other people is necessary when our personal motivation is more in the line of a wish than a resolve. For example, dietitians can help us understand how various foods affect us. They can outline a sensible diet for us and provide support in our struggle by having us report our progress or lack of it on a regular basis. They can suggest dieting aids such as keeping a log of what was eaten at each meal along with its caloric content. Even informal groups of people who are struggling with their weight can offer support to efforts to be temperate and reasonable in what we eat. Regular exercise also seems to help.

For those for whom alcohol or drugs are a serious problem, the various 12-step programs have proved most helpful. But these succeed only when a person admits that he or she is helpless in the face of the addiction and is willing to turn control over to a Higher Power. These people have to "hit bottom" and look to God and to a program or counseling for help.

To suggestions such as these, however, we should add prayer. It is not too petty to ask God for help in saying no when the urge to take one more piece of cake or one more drink is strong. The hunger and thirst within us, the empty place inside that we don't fill up with the pleasures of food and drink—this can be precisely where God is waiting to meet us.

Spiritual writers give other reasons to reinforce our weak wills. They speak of how the mind becomes so much clearer when the body is fasting. And experience shows this to be true.

They suggest that learning to control our appetite for food or drink is helpful in strengthening our efforts to tame other capital sins as well. This is particularly true with lust.

The desires of the body are like unruly horses that have to be tamed by some form of physical discipline. But strangely enough, keeping the desire for food or drink moderate and reasonable actually adds to the pleasure of eating and drinking.

For Reflection

1. *When you read or hear the word* gluttony, *what image comes to your mind?*

2. *What are some minor manifestations of gluttony you see at work in the lives of people you know? In your own life?*

3. *What practical suggestions do you have to tame the habit or impulse to eat or drink excessively, or even slightly, beyond the bounds of moderation?*

Prayer

O LORD, give me the strength to put my life in your hands and to say no to those things that are trying to control me.

▼▼▼▼▼▼▼

CHAPTER SEVEN

Sloth

▲▲▲▲▲▲▲

The slide in the confessional opened and a man's voice said, "Bless me Father..." Silence.

"How long since your last confession?" I asked.

"I don't know—three, four, five years," came the answer.

"What have you done?"

More silence. Then, "Nothin' Father. I'm a good Catholic."

Realizing that he was uncomfortable and might need a little help, I began to ask questions: "Do you go to Mass every Sunday?"

"Ah, Father, you know how it is. I work hard all week. I'm tired on Sunday, but I get there on Easter and Christmas. I'm a good Catholic."

"Did you eat meat on Friday?" This was back in the days when good Catholics were supposed to abstain from meat on that one day of the week.

"Ah, Father, you know how it is. I forget sometimes, but I'm a good man. I don't beat the wife."

I was sure I might get a positive answer on the next one: "Do you ever drink too much and get drunk?"

Once again, "No Father, but you know how it is. Sometimes when I'm out with the boys on Friday I have a few too many. Well, you know how it is."

I was desperate to find some sin or weakness that this "saint" in my confessional could admit to so I could give him absolution. "Do you say your prayers?"

"Ah Father, you know how it is. I get up early and am tired at night, but my wife she says hers."

Finally I asked him if he was sorry for any sin he might have committed. When he said, "Oh sure," I gave him a penance and absolution.

Perhaps this man did not know how to go to confession. Surely he did not seem to realize that he was spiritually lazy. He gave no evidence that his lackadaisical practice of his faith was due to anger with God or the Church. Nor did he indicate that shame or guilt had caused him to neglect his religious practice. He clearly had no intellectual problems about God, religion or the Church. He may even have been a hardworking, industrious husband and father. But the virus of sloth had infected his spiritual life.

Indifference to Others and to God

Webster's Ninth New Collegiate Dictionary (1994) defines sloth as "disinclination to action or labor: indolence." Sloth is different from taking it easy or slowing down at various times in our lives for a period of rest. Sloth is being lazy, idle, shiftless, without ambition *at times* and *in areas* where we have serious responsibilities: the worker who goofs off on the job, a student who always neglects homework, citizens who consistently fail to vote.

Sloth shows itself in small ways: not making the effort to answer a letter or return a phone call from a friend; putting off a host of small chores that need doing around the house. Physical inactivity, however, is but the *symptom* of the virus of sloth. The real infection is in the mind and in the soul. It lurks in our natural inclination to avoid obligations that require effort and commitment. It may well be a factor in the high divorce rate.

Marriages break up for many reasons. Some should have never been contracted. Irreconcilable differences do occur. But some break up because one or both partners are not willing to make the effort necessary to overcome whatever difficulties they are experiencing. They give in to the temptation of sloth.

Sloth can also exist in people who don't seem to be physically inactive at all. Those who are hardworking, ambitious and striving to get ahead can still be indifferent to responsibilities to family, needy neighbors, society and God.

Sloth works on the soul like a colony of termites on the foundation of a house. A single incident of neglect or indifference, like one termite, is in itself small and usually insignificant. But many small incidents gradually eat into the foundation of our heart-to-heart relationship with others and God. Once sloth takes hold, it becomes harder and harder to fulfill our responsibilities in a particular area of life.

If we neglect regular prayer, for example, and relegate participation in communal worship to Easter and Christmas, our relationship to the Church community and to God gradually dwindles away. If we consistently ignore the poor and needy, sloth hardens our heart to the needs and sufferings of others. If we put off time and time again calling a friend, the friendship may well die. It is important to name and claim the fainthearted attitude we take toward any of our duties or obligations for what it is: slothful inaction.

The causes of sloth are varied and hard to name because there can be legitimate reasons for not fulfilling our duty or obligation in a particular instance: sickness, lack of time, physical or mental inability to help and so on. Sloth, however, is avoiding or neglecting a responsibility *when we are capable of fulfilling it.*

Sloth lets less important projects or a more pleasing activity or our own leisure interests push a serious responsibility way down to the bottom of our list of priorities. In one parish with a thorough program for family participation in First Communion preparation, parents and children were required to come together for several evening meetings. Most parents were happy to be included. But a few complained loudly and did not attend. One was too busy taking his son to Boy Scouts and his daughter to ballet; this was just one more activity to take him out of the home at night. Another said he bowled the night of the sessions. The religious education of their children was not a high priority with these parents.

Our natural tendency to avoid activities that require effort and sacrifice is the breeding ground for the moral termites of sloth: wanting immediate solutions to problems and situations; refusing to accept that life is a struggle. After attending a talk on how to pursue a career in publishing, a young man in the audience asked how he could get a job as a senior editor—just like the speaker's. But when he was told that he had to start at the bottom with any type of job he could get, he said, "I don't want to do that. I want to start as a senior editor and work up from there."

The concept of consistent hard work with little or no immediate reward in order to achieve a future goal does not sit well with most of us. Our society places great value on satisfying the desire of the moment with the least possible effort. Forget the long, arduous road to some future good. If a project does not work out well at first, we tend to drop it and try something else. At times this may be the right thing to do, but often enough sloth is at work.

Sloth can be fueled by a feeling that we have failed to achieve the high ideals or the successful life we had imagined. It can cause us to feel "burned out" from too much work or pressure. It can cause us to lose hope, to slack off in our efforts, to become indifferent to the welfare of others. The resulting sadness causes us to become sluggish in meeting our obligations to others and to God.

The word *sloth* implies inactivity, languor, laziness. But it usually does not encompass one's total being. Hence we can be productive, busy, even a workaholic in some areas of life while lethargic in our care for our children or parents or spouse. Being too busy in some areas of life can also easily lead to ignoring our spiritual and religious development, resulting in spiritual indifference, carelessness and laziness. Any time for "those religious things" evaporates under the pressure of living and working in the "real world."

Change can fuel sloth. Layoffs, sickness, new or different working conditions, a divorce, as well as wars and political upheavals change the way we see life. The old does not seem to work. The new seems too difficult to learn or understand. We feel depressed, and that is the opening for the virus of sloth. Once the virus takes hold, we can all too easily decide the best solution is to do nothing.

Change also affects our pattern of religious thought and practice. In trying to cope with the fast-paced changes in our daily life, we can judge it is not worth the effort to try to deal with the changes occurring in the Church and in our own understanding of faith and God. Sloth takes hold of our spiritual life, and we become indifferent and cold.

The individualism that permeates our culture encourages sloth in a subtle manner. It tells us that each person has a right to think and act as he or she chooses as long as no one else is hurt. This attitude feeds intellectual and spiritual laziness. One becomes satisfied with one's own ideas and opinions on morals, values and fundamental beliefs without making the effort to discover and understand other points of view. Ideas expressed by those who may have a broader perspective or a fuller knowledge are dismissed as merely their "opinion." We don't want to make the effort to analyze, and perhaps change, our views on important issues.

Being comfortable with our lives can also feed sloth. Taking responsibilities to other people and to society seriously usually necessitates some change in us, some threat to our comfort. The more comfortable we are, the more we may be unwilling to open ourselves to the demands of change.

Factors such as low self-esteem or previous failure to assume and meet responsibilities may also activate sloth. The road to moral or spiritual laziness can be paved with a sense of guilt or shame as well as with the mistaken idea that we can never be forgiven by God for what we have done.

Finally, the changes that occur as we grow older often create a breeding ground for spiritual languor or lethargy. Sloth, someone has said, is the last shot the devil takes at us after all the other capital sins have been tamed. When passion has grown cold, when appetites are no longer ravenous, when little exciting or challenging seems to be on the horizon, when ambitions have been achieved or have proven impossible to achieve—this is when regrets over failures and lost opportunities gnaw at us. While such conditions can be present at any time in life, they seem most common as one ages. Instead of using whatever time one has left to become more concerned about the things of the spirit, the slothful person becomes more indifferent, even despairing.

Sloth in itself is a *temptation*. What we do about it leads to sin or to a growth in love and virtue. The stakes are high.

The harm done by the slothful person is sometimes obvious: Fathers do not support their children, so both the mother and the children live in poverty. Parents do not emphasize active involvement in their children's education, so the kids do not learn what they need to make their way in life. A company suffers financial loss because indifferent workers in one department slow work in other departments and eventually important deadlines are missed.

At other times the effects of giving into sloth are not so obvious. When people expect action from us and we don't come through, confidence is destroyed. Indolence and laziness breeds distrust among people. Walls go up not because of what is done but because of what is *not* done.

Sloth, like all the capital sins, is a perversion of love. It places our own ease or desire above our responsibility to another. Such indifference to our responsibilities is the opposite of love. Each time we neglect even small responsibilities—to a spouse, a neighbor, an employer, our country—our hearts harden and the distance between us and others increases.

To appreciate the real malice of sloth, we need to focus on the meaning of love and the impact sloth has on loving relationships. John Powell says that love means making the health, welfare and happiness of the other as important to us as our own health, welfare and happiness. In her book *In Good Conscience*, Sidney Callahan puts it this way: "Love is joyful interest with a predisposition to attend, approach, unite with and care about the love object."

The destroyer of love is not hate but indifference. We let the needs and wishes of the other become subordinate to our own. We stop caring.

When one "hates" another, there is still some connection, even some desire for a loving connection. When one is indifferent to another, there is no connection at all. The other is not important enough to be concerned about.

Indifference to others is also indifference to God. Jesus pointed out the eternal consequences of such indifference when he described how the Son of Man at the Last Judgment will separate the goats from the sheep based on what they neglected to do for others (see Matthew 25:31-46). Jesus also told the story of the rich man who was condemned not because he harmed poor Lazarus who lay hungry and sick at his gate but because he *ignored* him (Luke 16:19-31).

The second part of Webster's definition of sloth is "spiritual apathy and inactivity." This suggests how sloth infects the lives of people who profess a belief in God by convincing them to settle for a mere avoidance of sin instead of taking positive steps to grow in relationship with God.

Sloth produces lackluster Christians, cultural Catholics who merely go through the external motions with no enthusiasm for their religious practice. Sloth helps explain why Sunday attendance is only a fraction of total membership, why so few participate in prayer groups or Bible study, why so many are uninvolved in service to the needy.

But sloth can also infect those who attend Church regularly and make an effort to put faith into practice. It creeps in as a feeling of weariness with spiritual practices and tempts us to say, "Church and religion are boring. They offer me nothing." This attitude can then lead to jettisoning all efforts to be in contact with God. Ultimately it can lead to despair.

It is not easy to pinpoint the cause of spiritual sloth in an individual's life. It may be related to the intellectual sloth that keeps them from thinking about fundamental questions such as what gives meaning and ultimate purpose to life. It may be they have not made the effort to cultivate an adult understanding of and appreciation for their faith. It may be they have neglected to make the effort to work out their difficulties with the Church's teachings. Spiritual sloth may also take root in a tight daily schedule that leaves no time for "spiritual" or "religious" activities. The spiritually slothful person becomes like a ship without a rudder, floating aimlessly on the sea of life at the mercy of any wind or current that comes along.

Sloth is not necessarily the diagnosis, however, whenever we feel bored with religion and worship or whenever we merely go through the motions or pray without much thought. Some periods of dryness, some dark nights of the soul are times of purgation, of purification of one's desires and ambitions in climbing the spiritual ladder. They are an essential part of the spiritual journey. The great mystic Saint Teresa of Avila found little or no joy, comfort or consolation in meditation for something like fifteen years, but she kept at it until a spiritual breakthrough occurred.

Spiritual sloth is different than a lack of consolation and fervor in prayer. It is the apathy and laziness that keep us from being deeply involved with God. The most virulent form of this sin is best described by Evelyn Waugh, "Sloth is the condition in which a man is fully aware of the proper means of his salvation and refuses to take them because the whole apparatus of salvation fills him with tedium and disgust."

'I Just Don't Care!'

Because sloth has such negative connotations people have a hard time owning up to its presence. They may admit that they are careless or slow in meeting their responsibilities, but they will usually say they intend to do better. Sloth, like all the capital sins, is a master of disguise, extremely adept in attributing its lethargy to someone or something outside itself.

Claiming sloth begins by looking at our responsibilities and identifying those we neglect or fulfill in a slovenly manner. Next we need to be honest about the reasons we have for not acting, or for acting in a careless manner. This process requires a serious look at our responsibilities and the priority we give to each one. Each of our general categories of responsibilities—such as the education of children—will have subcategories with greater or lesser priority. Religious education will rate higher, for example, than driver's ed.

Finally, we need to examine the excuses we give for not fulfilling an obligation and make an honest judgment as to their legitimacy. People who slack off on the job may say it's because they are not paid enough. Parents will push responsibility for religious education onto the school. Men who neglect child support tend to blame the system for being unjust. Excuses such as, "It's not my responsibility," "I'm too busy," "Let someone else do it" require us to take another look at the priority we give our responsibilities in a given situation.

The need for rest or for time to oneself can be a perfectly good excuse for not doing something. But it can also be a cloak for sloth.

Sloth in one's religious obligations also seeks to place the blame on something else: "The Church is only interested in money." "The sermons are terrible." "I have to work sixty hours a week and have no time for this religious stuff." All are excuses for indifference to spiritual matters.

Sloth seldom manifests itself in an outright abhorrence of things religious and spiritual. It usually does not deny that these things are good and necessary. It will say that they are good for someone else—just not for me.

Keeping Love Alive

Sloth can take no root in a heart where love for life, neighbor and God is strong. Where there is love, there is always hope for an exciting future. Where there is love, there is joy and excitement. We need only think of the faces of people, young or old, when they see or talk about the one they love.

Love does not allow one to sit back listlessly. It moves one to do things for and with the loved one. It inspires people to share their happiness with others. Cultivating one's faith, hope and charity is the best insurance against sloth and the best cure for it.

People with a strong, vibrant spiritual life are not content to sit back and take it easy. They are constantly, according to their ability, busy about the Lord's work and they are content and joyful in these efforts.

Besides those things that foster growth of faith, hope and love, a few simple practices can help control the termites of sloth. First, it is necessary to tackle our natural inclination to take the easy way out when faced with a hard, boring or unpleasant task. When we are tempted to sit back and ignore something we know we should be doing, we must simply *do it* immediately.

Writing a list of things to do and people to see can be a powerful reminder of our obligations. Thinking of the consequences to ourselves and to others if we fail to meet a justified expectation on our list is often a motive to get moving when sloth is eating at us. Careful examination of the excuses we give for our inactivity will help us distinguish between legitimate reasons and those that are a cover-up for sloth.

What do we do if we realize that sloth has all but paralyzed our spiritual efforts? First, we need to remember that God has not given up on us and is always reaching out to us, waiting for us to come home. Second, we need to reflect on our vision of life and ask ourselves what is really important in the long run. This review of goals and priorities can be helped by talking to someone deeply in love with God or at least well-versed in the spiritual life. A successful businessman who had little time for religion called a priest one day and asked to talk about "this God stuff" because he had begun to realize that something was missing in his life.

Reading and reflecting on the Gospels will also help us realize that a life centered on love of God involves more than external practices. It is a matter of a heart trying to beat in tune with another heart—that of Jesus. The Gospels teach us the melody: unconditional love of all, even our enemies, and unconditional forgiveness, especially of our enemies. They also teach us the haunting grace note of suffering, as Jesus did even unto death on the cross.

Sloth deadens that gospel melody. It seduces one to listen to the deceptive siren song of sensual pleasure and comfort, to give up the joy of God for the joy of the world.

Reading spiritual books, joining with people who are actively searching for a better spiritual life—all can help overcome spiritual sloth. Regular daily prayer for enlightenment, courage and constancy is, of course, necessary to master the torpor that causes us to be bored with or indifferent to our obligation to know and worship God better and to reach a helping hand out to others.

In the long run, *taking action* wherever the termites of sloth are at work is the only way to wipe them out.

For Reflection

1. *A person who is "taking it easy" or "being laid back" can be manifesting sloth or acting in a legitimate, prudent manner. How would you discern the difference?*

2. *What are some manifestations of the termites of sloth at work in people's daily lives? In your own life? What effect do they have on relationships with other people?*

3. *When have you felt slothful in your relationship to God? How did you overcome this spiritual laziness or indifference?*

Prayer

GOD OF POWER AND MIGHT, send us your Spirit with a fire of wisdom to inspire us and a mighty wind to move us into action so we can joyfully do your work in this world.

CHAPTER EIGHT

▼▼▼▼▼▼

Lust

▲▲▲▲▲▲

The young woman was devastated. She had just learned that her boyfriend, with whom she had been having sex, was going to marry another woman who was carrying his child. She felt betrayed. He had been so profuse in his expressions of love for her. She was upset and angry and felt used. He had not really been interested in her as a person, she concluded, but had used her only to satisfy his selfish craving for momentary pleasure.

When he broke the news, he said that he had to do the "right" thing. It didn't seem to occur to him that what he had been doing with these two women had not been the right thing, that he had been harming them all along.

Most likely neither this young woman nor her boyfriend had ever considered fully or thoughtfully the function of sex in their growth and maturity as persons. Nor had they reflected very seriously on the limited role sex plays in the expression of true love.

When asked if she now thought that having sex with this young man had been wrong, she giggled and said, "Not really! It felt so good." To this outsider, at least, it seems as though both this young woman and her boyfriend were blinded to the purpose and deeper meaning of sex and love by the capital sin of lust.

Yet it is not hard to understand why they had been sleeping together. Our culture equates sex with love and says that this is the way to express affection. Movies and TV show the girl and the guy in bed or in a passionate embrace as soon as they begin to feel the first stirrings of attraction and affection. It is difficult to read a murder mystery or any novel without encountering a passionate love scene, usually with a person other than a spouse. Living together without the bonds of matrimony is so common that it scarcely even raises an eyebrow.

'Having Sex' Versus 'Making Love'

The *Oxford English Dictionary* defines lust as "desire, appetite, relish, inclination." As such, this desire is morally neutral. One can have a healthy lust for life or for adventure. One can also have an intense desire for a piece of art or a particular style of house. Usually, however, the word refers to the sexual urge.

Because sex is a gift from God, sex is *good*—just as are intellect, free will and imagination. But like all the other gifts God has given us, it needs to be used within reasonable bounds.

The sexual inclination varies in intensity in different people and at different times in each life. Often it requires drastic efforts to control. One of the hermits living in the desert in the fourth century suffered such severe sexual temptations that he would roll around naked in a patch of thorn bushes. This is not a recommended method of keeping the sexual urge in check, but it does show the intensity both of his temptation and of his resolve to control it.

The intense desire for sexual satisfaction becomes inordinate or immoderate when it leads to thoughts and actions that exceed the limits reason and nature have placed on sex. These limits take several forms.

First, they pertain to the *object* of one's desire. It is good to desire a spouse, but to desire the spouse of another is off limits. Jesus put it very bluntly: "You have heard it said, 'You shall not commit adultery.' But I say to you, everyone who looks at a woman with lust has already committed adultery with her in his heart" (Matthew 5:27-28).

There are also limits to the *means* one uses to satisfy this inclination. It is not unreasonable to enjoy the sight of a spouse's body, but pornography is another matter.

Masochistic or sadistic ways of arousing or satisfying our sexual urge are not reasonable either.

Finally, there are limits on the amount of *time* one spends thinking about and enjoying sex. Having sex constantly on one's mind and interpreting everything that happens in life through the lens of sex is certainly unreasonable.

These limits are not imposed in an arbitrary manner by some external authority. They reside in our human nature itself. Our sexuality embraces all we are, all we think and all we do. It enhances, develops and expresses our identity as men and women—same but different, independent but complementary. It calls us to respect and relate to other people—especially those of the opposite sex—in a loving, caring way.

The sex act is but one aspect of our human sexuality. It is intended, of course, to keep the race in existence. It is also an important means by which human beings grow in their manliness and womanliness and by which they express and grow in fidelity, commitment and caring.

Because the sex drive is so strong, however, it has a tendency to seek satisfaction in ways that are not consonant with human nature. This tendency is the capital sin of lust.

Every capital sin, as a perversion of love, deters our growth as human persons. It directs our love down a wrong path—a self-seeking, selfish path that puts one's own needs, security, pleasure and happiness above that of the other.

In specific situations it is not always easy to recognize that an *inordinate* desire is at work. We have already seen how greed, anger, sloth, envy, pride and gluttony can easily slip into our lives and pass themselves off as some very legitimate good such as security, health, needed rest or self-esteem. Lust is no exception.

Lust not only disguises itself as love but proclaims it is *real* love, the only kind of love that counts. The fact that the phrase "to make love" has become our society's euphemism for genital intercourse plays right into that deception.

Yet "having sex" is but one facet, and not the most important, in creating and expressing love. Fidelity, commitment and caring are by far more important. Sex in conjunction with these building blocks and in tandem with self-sacrifice, listening and communicating, affirming and supporting the other are what really "make" love. Without these other elements, the sex act weakens and ultimately destroys real love. Without these other elements, the total giving of one person to another symbolized by the sexual embrace is a lie.

Lust is the tendency to satisfy our sexual impulse without the other complicating elements of love. This is a perversion of love, not an expression of it.

Lust has its own unique way to justify its masquerade as love. It picks one aspect of this beautiful and complex reality and shouts, "See, this is love!" It argues that sex is a good and pleasurable gift from God and asks how can it be wrong. It ignores or trivializes other aspects of love's mosaic: getting to know and appreciate one another; being committed and faithful; being open and vulnerable; and subordinating one's own needs and desires to the needs and desires of another.

Lust refuses to see that, at times, love can and does exist between a man and woman without genital sex. A teacher of high school boys asked a group for a definition of love. All defined it in one word: *sex*. Further discussion revealed that they thought if one felt attracted to a young lady, "loved" her, having sex was the normal and ordinary way to show it.

People readily see that there is something unreasonable about an inclination that leads one to rape, to sexually abuse a child, to harass another sexually or to find satisfaction in pornography. It is more difficult, however, to put one's finger on other activities and say lust is at work.

One reason is that other desires or impulses may be operating. A woman may flirt because she wants to seduce a man or simply because she would like him to notice her and pay attention to her. A man may tell dirty stories because they excite him or simply because he wants to be one of the crowd.

Another reason is that sexual material is so pervasive in our society that one is not conscious of its impact. Lust has a public relations team second to none working for it. Chief among its agents are advertising and entertainment.

Implicit or explicit sex sells. Beautiful women in bikinis sell everything from soap to automobiles. Some ask what is wrong with this type of advertising. They claim it does not motivate them to go out and be unfaithful. In fact, they say, it does not even arouse them or affect them.

If that is so, one wonders why so much money is spent on this type of advertising. In fact, this constant flood of erotic material deadens people's sensibilities to the stirrings of lust within them.

Perhaps it is not as difficult to recognize the impulse of lust at work in those who buy magazines such as *Playgirl* or *Playboy*, or who view sexually explicit videos, or who frequent bars where the waitresses are scantily clad or topless.

A third reason people have a difficult time naming certain tendencies and inclination as lust is their difficulty foreseeing any negative effects of using sex merely for pleasure. They can't see how the desire for sex between consenting adults, single or married, can ever *in itself* be inordinate. A lie may be involved or an injustice done in such a relationship, but they see nothing unreasonable in satisfying their sexual urge as long as no one is "hurt." They reject the arguments from natural law as to the purpose of sex and make no attempt to understand them. Any sexual taboos are rejected as holdovers from another time.

But constantly satisfying our sexual desire without the presence of those elements that define committed love only enhances our selfishness. Such behavior directs our thoughts and energies toward satisfying our own pleasures and away from tackling the complexities of a mature human love relationship.

A young Lothario who bedded anyone who was willing was asked by his mother how he thought his cavalier attitude might affect an eventual marriage. "Oh, that will be different," he said. "Then I will be faithful." As yet he has not found the one woman worthy of his faithfulness. Nor can he know what he will do when the bloom of marriage wears off and the stress of daily living together builds.

Another negative effect of permitting lust to separate sex from the more complex demands of love is that this can weaken our desire for the things of the spirit. Lust tends to make one skeptical of the admonitions in Scripture and the teaching of the Church about the right use of sex. In its effort to justify itself, lust can cause one to develop an aversion to God.

Judeo-Christian philosophers may not have always agreed on what actions are expressions of lust, but they have agreed that in certain circumstances there can be something inordinate, unreasonable and perverse in one's desire for sex. They have also seen how lust is a root from which other kinds of sin spring. Many of these sins do not seem, at first glance, to be directly related to lust. Yet lying about one's love, or using violence, anger or fear to obtain consent from another has its source in lust. The young lady mentioned above felt hurt by her affair not because of the sexual acts involved but because of the young man's lies and betrayal.

Marriage is no guarantee that one is not acting from lust. Lust can exist in marriage. It is not the passion, the excitement, the pleasure that makes the sexual act lustful; it is the intention. Sexual ecstasy with the intent of mutually giving one's self completely to the other and thereby achieving not only union of body but also of mind and soul is honest, self-giving love. But using a spouse merely for one's own sexual pleasure without sharing a union of mind and thought smacks of lust. There may be affection, but it is self-seeking, not self-giving. There may even be commitment and faithfulness, but the well-being and happiness of the other is not the primary concern. Seeking one's own pleasure at the expense of, or without consideration of, the other—even a spouse—is a distortion of love.

'No More Sexual White Lies'

Claiming our sexual inclinations as a perversion of love, as lies, is difficult. Our ability to do so will depend in great part on our understanding of when sex is reasonable and our willingness to tell ourselves the truth when these limits are exceeded. Sorting this out is made all the more complicated because sex in itself is good, holy and so pleasurable.

Persons who cannot see the lie in premarital or extramarital sex between consenting adults are not likely to label as lustful their inclination to see everyone of the opposite sex as a possible bed partner. An unmarried person who draws a distinction between recreational sex and committed sex will likely not admit any thoughts and feelings as lust. He or she sees recreational sex as satisfying desire without any further responsibility to the other—merely two people having an enjoyable time together with no strings attached.

Others will not recognize and own lust because they maintain that chastity is out of date, a holdover from less enlightened cultures. Still others will claim controlling a natural desire is unnatural and makes one neurotic—despite the many examples of well-balanced people who are chaste both in and out of marriage. Many psychiatrists and psychologists, in fact, are on lust's public relations team. They suggest that patients indulge in sex outside of marriage for reasons of "mental health" and "developing fully as a person."

Finally, those who see erotic material merely as an art form or as entertainment are unlikely to admit to lustful impulses. After all, art and entertainment are meant to be enjoyed!

All of these rationalizations attempt to put a good and honest face on inclinations that are, in fact, inordinate and unreasonable. They make it difficult to easily and honestly admit that lust is active in our lives.

Applying the Bridle of Reason

The fastest and strongest horse in the world is of little use in a million-dollar race if it has not been broken to the bridle and is not under the control of a jockey who paces and guides it around the track. The sex drive is like that horse—very powerful, very wild. It needs to be tamed. It needs a controlling guide, reason.

Simply trying to ignore or deny one's erotic thoughts and feelings does not work. Suppressing them usually causes passion to surface in other, often destructive ways. Praying that we be delivered from these inclinations or temptations usually does not work unless we also take some steps to develop our self-control.

The first step, as always, in taming a capital sin is admitting that the inclination or desire for sex that we are feeling in this circumstance or with this particular person or in this manner is askew, inordinate, out of line. Along with this first step, here are other things we can do to help tame the virus of lust when it is actively infecting our lives.

We can ask God to enlighten us about the unreasonableness of our desires and to give us the strength we need to tame it. For Catholics this help is easily available in the sacraments of Penance and Eucharist.

We can ask ourselves questions similar to these:

- What kind of person would I like to be? Open, giving, loving? Or closed, selfish and taking?

- What kind of person am I becoming if I continue to give in to this impulse?

- Am I becoming the kind of person *God* wants me to be?

- How would I act if I were the person I would like to be?

- What is the effect of my actions on others?

We can look for support and guidance. At times the advice of someone who has experienced the struggle is helpful. There is the story of the girl whose father told her that she had to be home from her date by eleven. When she asked, "Why? Weren't you young once?," he answered, "That's why you have to be home by eleven!"

A wise mentor or counselor—especially a good spiritual director—can guide and support us in our efforts to grow in our capacity to love in a healthy, balanced way. He or she can also help us find the answers to questions such as those above as well as to any questions about why certain forms of sexual gratification are wrong.

We can also turn to the wisdom of Scripture and the teachings of the Church for enlightenment. These are not the dictates of a remote God sitting on a throne trying to frustrate human beings or the rantings of dried-up churchmen who want to take the fun out of life. They are guidelines on how to grow in our capacity to love more fully and grow in union with another. They are guidelines that grew out of the experience of human beings who have struggled with lust as we all do.

We can practice the suggestions of the great spiritual masters who recommend some form of self-denial in other areas of our lives, such as eating or drinking, in order to discipline the lustful impulse when it stirs. They all recommend simple practices such as averting our eyes from people, pictures, shows that incite lust and avoiding situations that give rise to lustful urges.

Finally, we can take steps to develop the virtues of modesty, chastity and continence to keep our lustful impulses at bay.

For Reflection

1. *How would you define lust?*

2. *What are some of the things in our society that arouse lust?*

3. *Reflect on a specific movie or TV show. What is the attitude toward casual sex or adultery it portrays? What is your reaction to this attitude?*

4. *What do you think of the statement, "Lust can exist in marriage"?*

Prayer

LORD, thank you for the gift of sex. Please give me the wisdom to know its proper place in my life and the strength to keep it in that place.

▼▼▼▼▼▼▼▼▼▼▼▼▼▼▼▼▼▼▼▼▼

GOING PLACES, Growing in Love

▲▲▲▲▲▲▲▲▲▲▲▲▲▲▲▲▲▲▲▲▲

When I told people I was writing a book on the seven capital sins, they would ask, "Why?" Eventually, after various attempts to explain, this answer became my standard: Because we can't grow in the spiritual life unless we acquire an accurate knowledge of those tendencies within ourselves which militate against that growth. And these tendencies are the seven capital sins.

Today there are numerous programs in spirituality. Some teach methods of meditation and prayer. Others foster self-development. All of this requires a continual examination of the behavior, motives and ideas which open us to or block us from loving ourselves, our neighbors and God. This examination requires us to name accurately what we have done, to accept our own personal responsibility for it and, finally, to do what we can to tame or overcome the tendency or temptation. To name, claim and tame these tendencies is what this book is all about.

This ongoing process of naming, claiming and taming needs to be done slowly, calmly, patiently, one day at a time. That way patterns, both good and bad, emerge. These patterns—our daily moral decisions—reveal who we are and who we want to be. But at the same time they are shaping our self-understanding and our goals. This circular process can be vicious and destructive if we do not take the time to identify the deadly habits and sinfulness which are at work.

Categories such as "the seven capital sins" can be helpful in discovering the predominate way or ways we are straying from the path of love. This way of classifying the destructive forces in our lives is not as popular as it once was. For one thing, people today are more likely to look to psychology or sociology for the causes of these problems than to seek the roots within their own souls. Then, too, there is the general distrust of religous language and ideas. Words such as *temptation, sin* and *guilt* are definitely out of fashion. But the realities they point to still exist in each of us. They still hinder us from leading full, loving lives. They still seduce us onto destructive paths.

These seven deadly tendencies are rooted in everyone's heart to some degree. Like viruses, they can flare up with the slightest provocation. They can never be cured or eradicated entirely, but they can be kept under control. The discipline needed to do this can also help us grow in virtue and in love.

It is important to remember that these deadly tendencies can engender other sinful thoughts, words, deeds or omissions. The guilt associated with a "capital sin" is an entirely different question from naming and claiming and taming it. It is also a different question from the causes of these viruses.

Traditional theology placed the cause in "original sin." Modern psychology looks at such things as environment, home life, genetic inheritance. Certainly these factors need to be given serious consideration.

Because the capital sins are at the root of all vices, or bad habits, they are also closely related to the virtues, or good habits, which develop by taming these destructive tendencies in our lives. These virtues have been treated here in rather summary fashion. They require an entire book of their own.

Going Where You Need to Get

Another question I was asked frequently when people heard I was writing this book about the seven capital sins was "What are they?"

A man in one of my groups came up with this simple memory aid: GOING PLACES. It plays off the idea that

90

capital sins lead us off the path of love, and then the letters in the phrase remind of the individual sins: The "G" in *GOING* stands for gluttony, and the letters in *PLACES* stand for the other six: *Pride, Lust, Anger, Covetousness* (greed), *Envy* and *Sloth*. These are the stumbling blocks, the detours, the dead ends along the path of life. Controlling and taming them hastens us along that path.

I hope this book helps you "go the places" you most want to go.

Bibliography

Fairlie, Henry. *The Seven Deadly Sins Today*. Washington, D.C.: New Republic Books, 1978.

Farrell, Walter, O.P. *A Companion to the Summa, Volume III: The Fullness of Life*. New York: Sheed and Ward, 1940.

Schimmel, Solomon. *The Seven Deadly Sins: Jewish, Christan and Classical Reflections on Human Nature*. New York: Oxford University Press, 1997.

Steinbacher, John. *The Seven Deadly Sins and Why We Love Them*. Riverside, Calif.: A Cancer Federation Book, 1994.

Wilson, Angus, et al. *The Seven Deadly Sins*. New York: Quill/William Morrow, 1992.

"The Seven Deadly Sins," *Parabola* (Winter, volume X, number 4, 1986).